GILBERT SPENCER, R.A.

MEMOIRS OF A PAINTER

By the same Author

*

STANLEY SPENCER

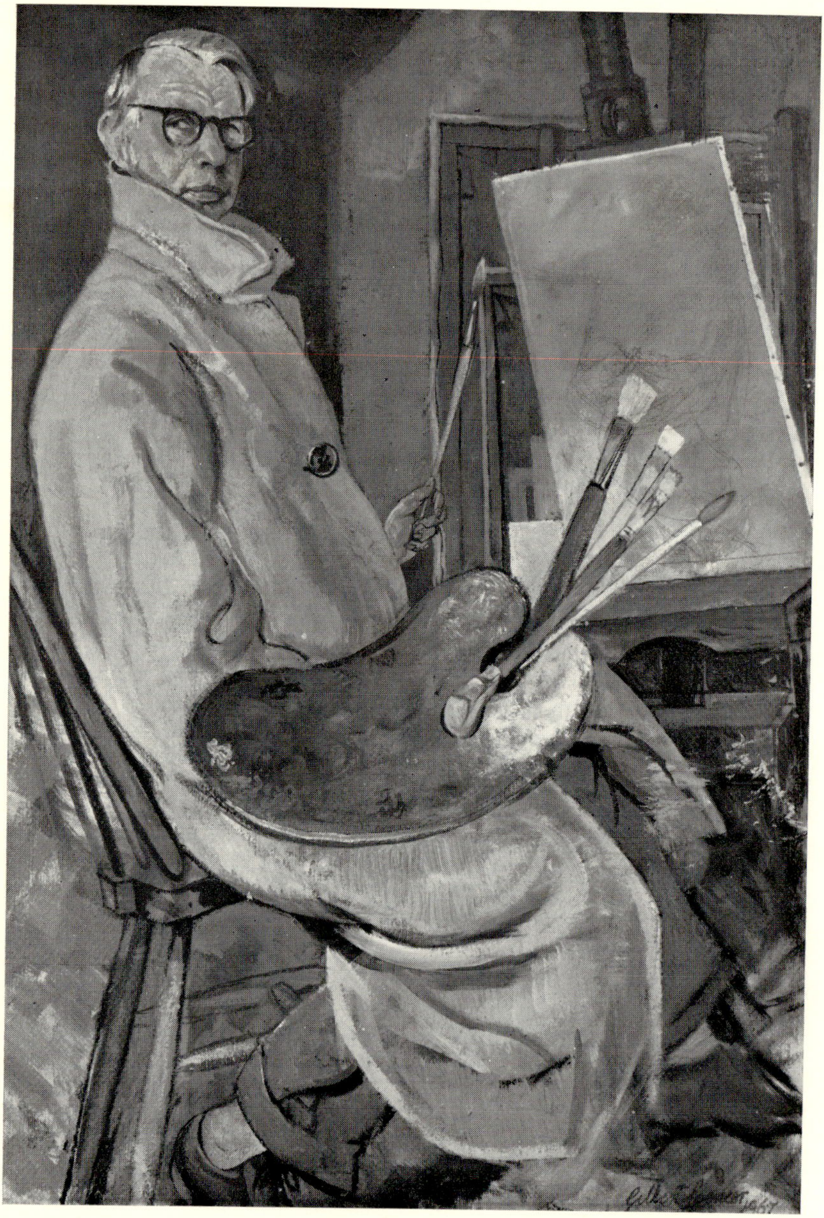

Self Portrait (1967)

GILBERT SPENCER, R.A.

MEMOIRS OF A PAINTER

1974

CHATTO & WINDUS

LONDON

Published by
Chatto & Windus Ltd
40 William IV Street
London WC2N 4DF

*

Clarke, Irwin & Co. Ltd.
Toronto

ISBN 7011 2030 4

Printed in Great Britain by
Ebenezer Baylis & Son Limited
The Trinity Press, Worcester, and London

FOR MY GRANDSON

ACKNOWLEDGEMENTS

It would be unfitting not to acknowledge my indebtedness to Mrs. Catherine Martineau for her constant help, and to her husband (Jack), and indeed to their whole family, for the warmth of their hospitality and stimulating company throughout the writing of this book.

The author and publishers also wish to thank the following for permission to reproduce drawings or paintings:

Margaret, Marchioness of Aberdeen for 'Suffolk Waggon';

Viscount Astor for a detail from 'Christ Preaching at Cookham' by Stanley Spencer;

Balliol College, Oxford for two details from the Balliol Murals;

City of Manchester Art Galleries for 'Burdens with Melbury Beacon';

Mr. R. M. Martineau for 'The Rick Party';

The Royal Academy of Arts for 'Self Portrait';

The Tate Gallery for 'The Beginnings of an event in history: The Tolpuddle Martyrs' and 'Cotswold Farm';

The Warden of the Students Union, University of London for 'The Scholar Gypsy'.

The Fine Arts Society Limited for 'Garsington';

CONTENTS

ILLUSTRATIONS

1

Cookham

1892–1909

I WAS born at Cookham on August 4th 1892, one year, one month and four days after my brother Stanley and the youngest of my parents' twelve children. Clearly my father only undertook the task of entering our names in the Family Bible late in life, and long before he reached my name at the bottom of the list he had wearied of filling in our birthdays. By the time I came along the high hopes, the influential connections and comparative prosperity of the vigorous early years of my family's life had largely vanished; and it is not surprising that my sister Annie, on whose shoulders the care of the two youngest of us mainly fell, stamped her foot indignantly when I was born.

For the next few years the nursery was to become as much her world as ours. The floor was bare except for a large tin of buttons going back to Waterloo, and a faded pink jigsaw puzzle of a map of the Crimea, but Annie's folded cut-outs were far preferable; the more she folded, the more we liked it. She was no doubt responsible for the paper nuns which Stan sent in procession round the room, under the cribs and bed, and back again. How they got through the barrage of non-conformity downstairs I do not know. I early set out on my own course of amusement with paper, pins, card-board boxes, and scissors making my farms; while

Stan used a branch from a fir tree, which our elder brother, Percy, had tied to the end of the bed, in which to conceal his cut-outs of little figures, and fascinated himself peering in at them. The bareboarded simplicity of our nursery was very good for us, making us work hard at our own ideas, if only to get something to play with. Not that we suffered any lack of entertainment with so many in the family to visit us. Our brother Horace had not at that time developed his exceptional skill as a conjurer, but he and Percy filled in gaps for us with shadow animals, and birds by lamplight on the wall.

My most natural early remembrance of my mother and father arises largely as the result of occasional nightmares. My father would come in and carry one or other of us into their bed, where we would lie between them in a state of happiness and security unknown in later life. We would wake up next morning to find ourselves back in our cribs, but with our trust unshaken.

At a suitable age we began saying our prayers after Annie, simple to begin with, but complicated later by the addition of more and more relations who died or got into difficulties. Having put us to bed, Annie, who was a member of the Maidenhead Orchestral Society, would then prop her music up on the chest of drawers and practise the viola, while we would watch the shadow of the bow, up the wall, break its back across the ceiling, and back again. Downstairs in the dining-room, which was directly below the nursery, my father continued to receive piano pupils until long after the time we were supposed to be asleep.

While, in memory, I am trying to go to sleep, lulled by Annie's viola, and by the works of Handel, Beethoven, Schubert, Bach, Mozart, or even a song composed by my brother Harold called 'Give a man a horse he can ride', this seems the place to describe something of my family's musical background. As far as I know it began with my grandfather Julius Spencer, master builder, and village constable. He created and trained a choir from among the villagers, and travelled around the Home Counties with them, from time to time singing to the Duke of Westminster's house parties at Cliveden.

As a widower Grandpa later married a Miss Gosling from Seton who had taken a governess's position in the village, and by whom he had three children, my father, Uncle Julius and Aunt Lizzie. Later Grandma wished one of the boys to learn the organ, and, as the story went, unable to decide which she spun a coin, which came down in favour of Uncle Julius. My father cried so much that my uncle gave way, and went in for Law, and my father was placed under Mr. Thorn at Cookham for the organ.

In Grandpa's choir was Annie Slack, who became our mother. She was nicknamed 'Birdie' on account of her soprano voice, but she had also earned a name for herself for mimicry with which from a little girl upwards she had entertained the neighbours. This came in useful when on occasions a member of the choir was absent and she could spiritedly fill her or *his* place. I myself can remember times at home when she cheerfully took the bass part. She was the perfect mother, the rock on whom we all depended taking all the demands of her children in her stride; and yet Stan and I never kissed her goodnight—it was always Father we kissed when we went to bed.

If the brass plate on our gate was not strictly correct in describing my father as 'Professor of Music' this was soon straightened out as the family came along. The records of the Royal College of Music should show the names of William George Spencer (piano under Parry) and Harold Spencer (violin under Rivaz)—both interchangeable. To these were added Annie (viola), Percy ('cello), Florence (piano), Sidney (piano and organ), and of course my mother with her singing and dancing. After her death, Will wrote to my sister Florence from Cologne Conservatoire where he was Piano Master, 'Once when I was playing Schumann's Papillons Opus 2 in the dining-room at Fernley and had just reached the 4th Number, Mother came in from the kitchen and almost danced to it.'

Something akin to tragedy crossed the musical path of my brother Will. He had been early earmarked for a high destiny; we heard of him, an infant prodigy, in velveteens, his feet unable to reach the pedals, playing at Cliveden before the Prince of Wales, but my father's overbearing Victorian discipline led to a breakdown. He was sent to a hospital at Virginia Water, from which the family finances never recovered. But Will himself did, owing to my mother's determination and insight, sufficiently, in any case, to give concerts again in London, before going to Germany where he married and settled in Cologne. It was my father who never quite got over the failure of his highest hopes, burying himself and his disappointment more and more in his books.

Still his pupils came and went, and music remained the common language at home. We grew up with it naturally, and could listen and talk at the same time. The professional approach was vigorous and robust. Indeed, there was no challenge to music at home until Mr. Ernest Lumsden (the etcher and painter, and a pupil of Will's for the piano) noticed Stan's drawing of a sack of potatoes, which ultimately led to his going to the Slade. It is curious to realize now that throughout the period of my father's despondency and my mother's anxiety over Will, genius of an unlooked-for kind was quietly developing in its own good time under the same roof. Will's sacrifice on the altar of my father's Victorian theories and rigid training of the young was not in vain if Stanley's genius was left free.

Discipline to a lesser degree of course we had. Will who was of a serious as well as a humorous nature once found that Stan had broken what my mother never referred to as other than a 'certain article', and solemnly took him downstairs, saying, 'Stanley has come to confess'. We were not of the confessing kind, however, nor were scapegoats looked for in the family. Mother's method when pandemonium threatened was to open the door sufficiently to get her arm through, and make swishing noises with her cane, which she never used. Once when my father tapped me on the head and I began to cry she exclaimed reprovingly, 'Oh William!' and *he* left the room.

My father's technique at meal times was to sit as if he were one of us. Having said Grace he took no further part in carving or serving, leaving that all to my mother at the head of the table (she always served him first), and flinging himself freely into the tensions and arguments which between our elders seemed to be a digestive necessity at mealtimes. At the end of it all Father would turn his chair to the fireplace, place his napkin over his face, and go to sleep. Of course to begin with the talk was well over our heads, and Stan and I, often relegated to the side-table by the piano, were quite glad to 'get down' and run upstairs to prepare for our walks with Annie.

At first our concern on these walks was not to be left behind, calling after her, 'Wait for me, Annie', but as we grew older we hoped she would not notice that we were not following, but perhaps taking a look in the blacksmith's shop, until she was well across the moor. In fair weather the skies of Cookham were bright and strong, and against them the old red brick cottages and colour washed houses gave a cheerful welcome to anyone entering the village. Surrounded as we were by commons, streams, and backwaters, curtained off on the eastern fringe by Cliveden Woods, and shut off by the toll gate, we had the sense of being islanders. The lanes were well shaded by elm trees and here and there a high wall would conceal one of Grandpa's new houses, or some fine old lodge, largely mysteries to us hidden behind their walls and trees; but occasionally a gate would be left open, and we caught a glimpse through to the other side.

This love of our home and village played an important part in our development. Presumably it was passed on to us through our father. With so much of his life now in the past, it was all he had to give us, but it was all we needed, or for that matter ever wanted. On our first visit away we were taken to Furze Platt to stay with our brother Harold. A man playing a mouth organ below our window there was a poor substitute for the sound of instrumental music that came to us at home across the intervening gardens from the 'Kings Arms' on summer evenings.

At the Diamond Jubilee of Queen Victoria, when I was five years old, I have a clear impression of my brother and I leading a strange straggling procession of villagers, representatives none the less of an all powerful empire. We had been put in the front to prevent our being left behind. Looking at an old faded photograph of the event, I was able to remind myself of the clothes we were wearing, particularly the hats. We seem to have been dogged all our childhood by uncomfortable hats, and these were no exception, built-up with wires, draped with silk, and fringed with lace.

So far our education depended on Annie's reading to us, and Father occasionally dictating something out of the *Daily News* to test our spelling. On his London days he would purchase one of W. T. Stead's 'Books for the Bairns' published at a penny. It was through these that we enjoyed a splendidly mixed reading—*Brer Rabbit*, *Snow White*, *Don Quixote*, *Gulliver's Travels*, *Pilgrim's Progress*, *Tanglewood Tales*, and many others. Our Bible readings were ticked off on a card index supplied by the British & Foreign Bible Society of which Mother was the local secretary. One of these precious 'Books for the Bairns' series, like dear Baron Munchausen, might have been found at any time shut up in the leaves of our Bible, to mark the place.

Once a week as part of our curriculum we crossed the road to receive our first lessons in drawing and painting from Miss Dorothy Bailey. In our walks with Annie we had as little boys come across her father, Mr. William Bailey, builder and plumber, devotedly painting his pictures in and around the meadows and streams. He had passed this gift on to his daughter, and now in her turn she began to teach us to paint flowers from nature in water-colour. Around us, as we worked, were her father's pictures all painted in Cookham, of Cookham—we had two of them in our own house—and these weekly visits had a greater influence on us, and took on an importance which our elders at home had not foreseen. There, music, with literature only a little behind, held sway, and fine art was hardly in evidence at all, except for a little reproduction of Fred Walker's 'Geese in Cookham Village'. This picture and Mr. Bailey's pictures of Cookham inspired in us an early and distinct preference for local scenes which never left us.

Our leaning towards music was inevitable. I remember my mother calling to me from the kitchen urging me to practise, or I would be sorry one day. But I did not want to practise. My secret love, for I was shy, was trying to compose when Father was out of the way. Looking back, those secret visits to the piano to play my own tunes were only just less pleasurable than my joy in my painted models. I used to read *Grove's Dictionary*, and doted on the little contemporary drawing of Beethoven with the hat on the back of his head. I also deeply yearned to be found with the original score of Schubert's Unfinished Symphony in my pocket. There were always lurking in my head a dozen or more short keyboard melodies, and though I never knew what I was going to compose when I sat down at the piano, I went straight through with them. This love of composition might have been encouraged. Instead, Annie at that time was giving me piano lessons, and I was able to play a little Clementi and Dussek, but I dodged scales, and much as I loved to extemporize, my musical explorations went no further. Years later when I was married and we had a flat at the top of Mr. Fox-Strangways' house, he converted one of my tunes into a fugue, quite a page and a half of it; and in the war when the R.C.A. had moved to Ambleside, Edmund Rubbra came to give a concert and in conversation afterwards told me he had got one of my musical compositions. As it turned out he knew my lifelong friend Joyce Peters, for whom I had written it down as a boy. I had little idea how to write it, my crochets were nearly as large as my breves, except that I had given them legs, and blacked in their faces. No wonder Rubbra described it as rather a spidery affair.

Sunday was not a day of rest at home, with my father, Will, Harold, and often Sidney having to be got off to their organ lofts, before Stan and I could be got out of the way, with Annie, to church. As a staunch supporter of the Wesleyan Church, Mother was involved in a local crisis which at the time took up a lot of energy. Her dramatic accounts of meetings ended to our sorrow in the closing of the Cookham Chapel in favour of a new one at Cookham Rise, and the 'Risers' won a famous victory. Stan and I were at our chapel on the last Sunday for evensong before the doors were shut—(to open again in 1962 to house the permanent Stanley Spencer Memorial Exhibition). If we now changed buildings from chapel to church we did not change the form of our religion. We were unquestionably low church and had a strong family characteristic of rationalism and common sense which we could not forsake in pursuit of a mystical faith. Yet the Bible reading did its work. I still like to slip into Evensong at some village church and feel the better for it.

There was no alteration in our home life to disturb our contentment other than when Mother turned house decorator. In the midst of the confusion of her inexperience and determination Father yet contrived to read his books undisturbed. Nevertheless we were growing up, and a wind of change was blowing our way. Originally in the years before I was born, my father had set up in Cookham as a Schoolmaster, building a small classroom in Sammy Sandall's garden next door. With increasing demands on his time as a music teacher, he had transferred the school to the Miss Georges' who lived next door but one. Now they announced they were giving up the school, and, as good as their word, they soon left for Australia. Into the breach, to my parents' relief, stepped Annie and, for a time, my sister Florence. And so, our nursery days over, we found ourselves following Annie down the garden path to school. But a slight curbing rein was put on us. We were told that the two Miss Georges had changed to the two Miss Spencers, and that in school hours we were not to call them by their Christian names.

Our education would not satisfy today's requirements, or even, one would think, the requirements of those days. It was clear that there were no possible further economies which would have enabled my father to send us to a private school, and my mother's snobbish objections to the village school seemed sufficient to defeat the intentions of the 1870 Education Act, both for ourselves and the poorer élite of the village. The attendance was not large, so that each pupil drawn from a healthy middle class received individual attention, and they had plenty of individuality about them. One Jack Hatch, corrected by Annie for calling a bucket a 'bockert' conceded that he would say bucket in school but 'bockert' out. From a distance we could hear Father indoors giving his music lessons, but this counter-attraction for us lost its savour when we realized that if we misbehaved we would be sent to Mr. Spencer. This threat hung like the sword of Damocles over our heads, and caused Hilda Jemmett, an orphan, who was always dressed in black, to ask my sister whether 'that was what Mr. Spencer was kept for'.

For me the 'after tea' feeling, which was such a favourite period for Stan upstairs, would find me edging my way to one end of the kitchen table, with Alice, our maid, perched at the other end reading. Here I continued happily sand papering and painting my models of farm carts. Sometimes I wanted leather for the horse's harness and there behind the dresser curtain were rows of old boots and shoes spanning the whole of the Spencer family's life at Fernley. When it came to painting the carts, Stan would let me have some of his paints, and never minded if, like Oliver, I asked for more. I attach great importance to the colour of these models and included one in my retrospective exhibition at Reading Museum and Art Gallery, because I believe they were the foundation of all that made that exhibition possible. Like Stan's 'Sack of Potatoes'—and what prophet could have foretold what would come out of that sack—my farm carts were the writing on the wall for me.

2

Brixton

1910–1912

WITH my brother's departure to the Slade in 1909 came my first partial separation from him. However much I may have felt myself to be happily employed, my future did not appear sufficiently convincing to my elders. It was therefore decided at this late hour (I was sixteen) that some sort of general education away from home might help. Through personal recommendation, the Ruskin School kept by Mr. T. N. Evans at Maidenhead was chosen, and, as Stan left each morning for the Slade, I left with him to walk across the Strand meadows and through North Town to school.

In these days of psychology it would be regarded as criminal to have sent me there at all. It was a private mixed school and the pupils were all advanced and preparing for matriculation, but Mr. Evans was thorough and kind and tried hard to fit me in. As a snap question he asked the pupils what matter, if any, added to the earth's substance. Before anyone else could answer I called out 'A meteor, sir'. For a moment there was silence, then with a twinkle in his eye he placed his hand on my head, declaring to the whole school, 'Gilbert is right, Gilbert is right'. However in the end I returned home to all practical purposes, as I had left it.

There is no doubt that as the youngest member of the family, quite unnoticed by myself, I was becoming a problem. I was quite content to go on with my secret visits to the piano to play my own tunes, occasionally varying this by putting one of my brightly painted model carts on top of it. I gave no other signs as to my tastes at all. I seldom read books then, and would have felt a hypocrite to be seen with one, not pretending to join my elders in their passionate interest in literature. Instead I took to football on Cookham Moor and in this I rendered a service to Stan. Our eldest brother Will, as I have described, had been severely strained by my father's ambitious discipline, which left little or no room for recreation. Stan joined me on the moor, and in other outdoor pastimes. Years later he told me when he heard a football being kicked around on the moor he was tempted to put his palette down.

Plenty of people meanwhile were trying to help me and there came a suggestion from Mr. Price Jones, the 'chymiste' that I should write the labels for a lightning cough cure which he was concocting for the wheezy Cookhamites. It was a pity he did not visit me in his office earlier. I had printed about five hundred of them, and on each had written: 'One tablespoonfool'. One would think when my father heard of the disaster it might have disturbed him that at seventeen years of age I could have made such a mistake, but he joined in the general merriment.

My interest in Mr. Hatch's farm carts may have led Harold to suggest that a fruit farmer friend of his, living at Waltham St. Lawrence, might take me as an apprentice. Converted to a cap, cardigan, breeches, gaiters and a pair of tough boots, for about three months I cycled backwards and forwards each day, by which time it was apparent that fruit farming had no connection whatever with my underlying feelings.

Architecture, which involved a reorganization of my appearance, got no further than an interview to which I was taken by my brother Percy, and which was, as might have been expected, brief. For what could I say? My only experience of architecture was what Cookham, half a dozen of Grandpa's houses, and a visit to Windsor Castle, had to offer. After each of these failures I was quite content to return to the kitchen table with my carts. But at least my future failures were to be in the right direction for now my father putting by his books for a moment said, 'Gil might do something with his hands.' This suggestion was prompted by my carts on top of the piano, rather than by what I was playing on the keyboard below. Having given two sons to music he was not inclined to see his youngest treading on his favourite corn.

The first attempt to steer me in the right direction accordingly took me to Brixton to live in lodgings with Percy so that I could attend the Camberwell School of Art and Crafts, and learn woodcarving. Situated in the Peckham Road, it was a comparatively new building, splendidly solid, with an entrance supported by two Herculean figures. What I remember of Camberwell then has to be carefully sorted out if I am not to confuse those times with my own direction of the Department of Painting there forty years later. There were of course distinguished teachers but, as I was what would now be called a junior, I had little or no contact with them. I was chiefly under the direction of Mr. Smith, a smartish, almost military, type of man. His demonstrations were clever, but tricky. Under his guidance I drew David's eye, nose and mouth, but looking back now I think his methods made them too easy. Once a week he took us out on to a patch of grass behind the school where we were set to paint in water-colours what I thought to be the brewery, but which was in fact the chimney of the hospital. Owing to the size of the class he walked up and down behind us, occasionally adding a general instruction, one of which 'Shadows Blue' I again found too great a simplification, sending me straight into the ultramarine.

Stan once showed me how to draw a foot, and gave it up because he said mine was better than his, but when I did a water-colour of cows in the shadow of some trees, he did not like it. He said the cows were too blue and vulgar. If I had an answer to this it was Mr. Smith's teaching at Camberwell.

I occasionally saw the principal, Mr. Dalton, a gentlemanly sensitive man, in his room, with my work. Turning up a horse I had drawn he drew one himself on a separate sheet, which was neat, and helpful as instruction. I thought him brave to have drawn it with an indelible pencil.

Teaching in those days (and I am going back sixty years) was directed towards academic ideals, subtly introduced as the pupils advanced. We believed that our teachers knew, and that we did not. They earned their living teaching us, and we paid to listen to them. As a family we were obedient, and conscious of the relationship between master and pupil, this no doubt being encouraged by Father's teaching, even if at times his was rather harsh as when he told a pupil that she played the piano like one of her father's carthorses. But the danger in this was that a really bad teacher could have crippled us without anyone being the wiser. So far we had escaped those dangers. Our general education at home gave a measure of freedom to us not usual in school, and by the time I was sent to

Camberwell I had leapt over a number of stiles without noticing them.

The hours at Camberwell were long, and there were evening classes as well which I attended for wood-carving. I cannot remember the master by name, and can have made no impression on him as at the end of my first year I was told I was not returning. I was neither sorry nor ashamed, and suffered no guilt complex, but while I might have been hoping that my holidays at Cookham would now be never ending, Percy had tracked down another school which it was hoped might bring better results—the School of Art Wood Carving in Thurloe Place. I never knew the foundation of the school nor who paid for what, but I have the feeling that many of the pupils had been considered suitable to benefit from charities, the conditions of which were to be found posted up behind vestry doors in churches around the city, perhaps connected with City Guilds.

As a building it bore no resemblance to the splendidly solid outward appearance of Camberwell. It had been in private ownership in the past, and was housed in an old three-storied building which viewed from the road gave one the feeling of early Italian three-tier frescoes. Dimly one could see the pupils, all wearing white smocks, like angels, moving around, and God, in the form of Miss M. Reeks, in her office on the first floor above the basement shop. When one pushed open the door to enter, a bell rang just outside her room so that by the time one had climbed the stairs she appeared to glide out on to the landing as by some invisible propulsion. She was small, wore a blue smock, and must have been one of the first women to crop her white hair closely. She looked at one through gold rimmed spectacles. Those Victorian ladies become more, and not less, vivid with time, and their characters and dedication appear strengthened and all the more remarkable.

When Miss Reeks talked to me it was clear that she was as much concerned with my character as with my progress as a woodcarver—in fact more so. The classes she left to Miss Burton who was as large as Miss Reeks was small. She was in charge of the beginners, and, in spite of my year at Camberwell, I was such a one. She generally stood with her back to the window just watching us, and, for different reasons, visiting us at the benches. She visited me! I had sliced off a chunk of wood by accident. She first folded my hand round the chisel in the proper manner, and then guided me round what remained of my carving. I could see at once how much better it was than when I attempted it single handed.

There were other masters. Mr. Smith was in charge of the advanced pupils upstairs, and still more important, Mr. Grimwood, who might be described as the Tonks* of the school, though there was no need to be frightened of him. Picking up one of my tools, he examined it rather like cricketers sometimes lift up their bats and examine the face, particularly at the strike end. Having given it a little rub on the stone, he showed me some beautiful clean cutting which I saw was another way of drawing. Amidst my own uncertainties this kind of draughtsmanship shone like a good deed in a naughty world. I had not then sharpened my tools as later I came to sharpen my pencils.

I was well behaved—we had to be—for Miss Reeks's impregnable silence in her own room seemed to make

* *Henry Tonks (1862–1937). Member of the New English Art Club. Appointed Slade Professor (1918).*

itself felt throughout the school. But she thought I could not draw, and in due course I again found myself returning home, never to return to Brixton, although the vivid almost magical experiences of that time and place steal on me still.

It was not all magic. I early discarded some of my romantic illusions about going out into the world, and but for Percy, with whom I lodged, I very much doubt if I would have been out in the world for long. My brother had been living in London for some years before I arrived, and in his spare time had brought a kind of Dickensian inquisitiveness into his walks around Brixton and South London, which he now shared with me. I remember I was dumbfounded by the sight of a funeral with all its equestrian trappings—not unlike those in primitive paintings—in this case laid on by the undertaker, L. J. Prebble, on a wet November afternoon in the Brixton Road.

My own walks had started timidly enough. I used to pick my way down Cold Harbour Lane to Camberwell Green, occasionally varying this by taking a twopenny ride on one of Tilling's buses. By practise I became an expert at mounting them while in motion which was not unlike flinging oneself on to the roundabouts on Cookham Moor, or on to a moving gaily painted caravan. The short-lived trams were in their prime, but I seldom used them as they swayed and swerved about so frighteningly that I used to duck when they passed one another.

Rattray Road in general, and our lodging in particular has not altered materially in the years that have passed since I went to live there, even down to the special feature introduced into the porch by Mr. Curtis, our landlord, of white glazed tiles with two green bands. This was to distinguish No. 27 from the rest for the sake of his wife Lily, 'on one of her late nights', he would say archly, to which she would reply with mock indignation 'George!'

Besides my brother and myself there were three other lodgers. In those days you never spoke to your next door neighbour and if 'next door' happened to be the next room, it made little difference. Our next door neighbour was a lady of uncertain age, who spent much time making herself up before proceeding to her work in the city. Mr. Curtis was much amused by her, and referred to her as 'the lady of the redecoration'. The two gentlemen had only recently arrived from the north and had not yet acclimatized themselves to the Londoner's traditional reticence. At breakfast one morning one of them, Mr. Peat, who stood six feet four inches in his socks, commented out of the blue that 'the birds run small in these parts'.

London cries seemed to follow fairly traditional lines, but there was one 'Mena, Mena, Me' which drew me to the window. Looking out I perceived a big woman carrying on her arm a large basket of cat's meat. As she proceeded with her accompanying 'cry', doors began to open and shut, and cats of all kinds appeared simultaneously as from nowhere. With a deft technique of her own she flicked off appropriate portions from the end of a skewer right under their very noses, and passed on to my surprise, without waiting for any money. Later it was explained to me that they were 'account' cats.

I was myself controlled at that time by a financial discipline which included a black-lidded account book in which I had to log my daily expenses. I discovered that my taste for chocolate biscuits led me to discriminate heavily in their favour although I disguised this by entering them in my cash book as roast beef and two veg, until my subterfuge was disclosed by my spotty complexion.

I was quick to realize that here in Brixton we were in the heart of the struggle for survival. The red glare of the London skies killed the starry heavens shining over Cookham, but not the night life of the Brixton Road. Those were the days before cold storage, and it was a desperate time to walk down the Atlantic Road late at night, when the lean and hungry ones timed their visits to perfection. They knew the butcher's dilemma, as with each passing minute, they eyed his tumbling prices. By midnight the road was in uproar with high pressure bargaining. It was a cut-throat business, though no throats were cut. There was nothing sinister or sordid about it, just a spirit that was London's, with the evening shoppers swarming round barrows illumined by paraffin flares, and floating on a sea of indescribable litter, and the barrowmen themselves shouting their wares, and offering goods of little value to an intelligent and informed clientele. On one occasion Percy took me along to hear a man who was selling boot polish. The man's voice was affected, and sounded cultured, and towards the end, producing an odd shoe on which to demonstrate the qualities of the polish, he drew our attention to its 'nutritiousness'.

The noise and din of London then was an honourable one derived largely from horsedrawn wagons, sounding like the continuous recession of the sea over shingle. In the Brixton Road too there were instrumentalists whose music fought its way through the sound barrier to their caps acting as their box office on the pavements. They and the barrel organs may have been an encouragement to the horses in their pull up Brixton Hill. Waiting for them at the top was that most humane of London symbols then, the horse-trough—the petrol pump of those days. Just round the corner one might have observed the 'horse' of the future beginning to emerge in the shape of a four-wheeler that had had a kind of a heart-transplant to turn it into a car. The driver sat a little high for these days, but not so high as the cabbies he had succeeded. He steered often with one hand, and kept the other at the ready to sound his horn. We did not have to worry about him; we had not yet lost our status as pedestrians, and he was as yet a rare visitant who had to drive with the greatest of care.

Percy sometimes broke away from the colourful scene to take me to art galleries. I was not ready for them then, as a liking for looking at pictures was no incentive for me, and only emerged later with my own efforts to paint. But first there had to be Stan's fateful intervention which was the turning point in my life. As he returned to his room one day after dinner to continue painting, he said, 'I don't see why Gil shouldn't go to the Slade'.

3

The Slade

1913–1915

RECENTLY looking through old papers, I unfolded one and read, 'University College, Slade School of Fine Art, Spring Term 1913 – £5', signed C. Koe Child (Sec.). It should have read £10 but as I could only afford half, I was accepted there on a basis of three days a week. Thus armed, I set off to catch the ten minutes to nine train as Stan had done before me, wearing my fruit farming clothes complete with cap, breeches and gaiters. I don't remember feeling unduly nervous; I felt I had been at the Slade before, as in spirit I had.

I have already described in my memoir of my brother the Slade School as it was then. To wait outside Professor Brown's room could revive unhappy memories for those who had had earlier experiences of headmasters and entering it deepened the feeling of gloom. The room sadly needed redecorating, the walls were bare, and there was nothing to suggest the glory of the place. Brown sat at the table leaning back in his chair. Behind him stood Tonks and Steer, each with an arm stretched out laying along the mantelpiece. It was all so still that they might have passed for a tableau in Madame Tussauds'. Brown wore an ageing black frock coat, with here and there some smudges of paint on it. To be interviewed by him was not an encouraging experience;

one almost felt he hated the sight of students. His face seemed flushed with anger, and it was only later that one discovered that he suffered from a distressing shyness. A few mumbled words from him, on this my first introduction, and I found myself ascending the stairs on my way to the Antique Room.

There the room was full of students, but quiet, as the masters, Russell and Lees, were going round. Later I received a visit from Tonks who sat side saddle on the 'donkey' his legs crossed, and one knee cupped in his hands. When standing up he was tall with a slight stoop, and kept his hands holding on to the lapels of his coat. His entry into a room was authoritative but without 'side', his features giving the impression both of severity and sadness, but he had an easy conversational way with him, though it was always a monologue. He talked of dedication, the privilege of being an artist, that to do a bad drawing was like living with a lie, and he proceeded to implant these ideals by ruthless and withering criticism. I remember once coming home and feeling like flinging myself under a train, and Stan telling me not to mind as he did it to everyone, but not, I think, to Stan. It is a measure of Tonks's greatness and perception as a teacher that from the moment he saw Stan's drawing of the Cookham Fire Brigade on snails with its extraordinary power of concentration, he recognized what he had got in him and let him alone. Writing to Selwyn Image at that time he said the danger for Stanley was an overcrowding of ideas. Tonks was a discovery of Professor Brown at the Westminster School of Art. Brown persuaded him to give up his post as house surgeon at a London hospital, and to come to the Slade as a member of his staff.

I had already completed some antique drawings, in

marked contrast to my first life drawings, for which Roberts had warned me dryly 'You mustn't copy', when Tonks told me to draw (I am sure he never said 'copy') a Michelangelo reproduction. I took it home and worked very hard and hopefully at it, but Tonks was disgusted with it! It was then I realized the besetting dangers of imitation, and the significance of Roberts' warning.

Eighteen months later Brown told me I had won the Life Drawing Prize, but before I could thank him he added 'But you can't have it; you have not passed Perspective'. I had never seen an anatomy book nor a perspective book in my life, either in the Slade School or elsewhere. He told me to come to his room where he set me a problem. How much he knew of perspective I do not know, but I knew Tonks had done anatomy, and would be largely responsible for the award. I drew the cube out of my head and added the perspective as best I could. Craning his neck over it, and adding a few words, Brown initialed it 'Passed. F.B.'. and gave me my £10. To have won the prize without knowledge of perspective or anatomy was surely a victory.

At home the news was received with complacency, in which I shared. There had been much of this sort of thing, one way and another in the past. In miniature it was my brother's experience when he returned to tell Father that he had won the Slade Scholarship, but that he could not have it because the home-spun nature of his education did not fit in with university requirements. He made good by answering a few set questions with the same freedom with which I had approached my own problem.

From now on I felt I had graduated, and seeing these drawings again recently, I think I was justified in that conviction. I attribute it to those two vital years at the

Slade School of Fine Art. If I could then have set a motto over its entrance it would have read 'We teach you the spelling and leave you to make the sentences', and these sentences, grammatical or otherwise, were formed and shown up in monthly compositions or for special awards. Consequently there was nothing out of the usual for me to enter a picture for the Slade Summer Prize, but it surprises me now that, with the exception of my three murals, 'The Seven Ages of Man', now in the Hamilton Art Gallery in Canada, still remains the largest canvas I ever covered. I painted it in the barn over in Ovey's Farm, completely at home among my carts and wagons. To these I now added an elevator as the focus, round which I introduced the Seven Ages, using my brother Stanley and Peggy Hatch as the lovers, and Amy Hatch as the mother holding the baby.

When it was finished John Fowler and I carried it like a table to the station, and a few days later I followed in its wake to find it safely leaning against the wall awaiting the fateful day. Brown took the criticism, and we all stood round listening to his comments. He moved from one picture to another, stopping a bit longer at some than others. A tradition had grown up that the prize-winning picture was left to the last. Once he stood looking at mine, but said nothing, and continued on round. I pretended not to notice, but students began glancing in my direction, till at last there seemed no doubt about it as there were no pictures left to criticize but mine. He gave it for him an unusually encouraging criticism; and then just as everyone was preparing to clap, he broke right across tradition by returning to Ruth Humphries' picture and awarded her the prize, adding that he had decided to give me a consolation prize of £6.

A few days later Henry Lamb looked in to see the

prize entries, and at his kind invitation I sent mine to his studio in the Vale of Health Hotel, Hampstead, naming £20 as my price. Lamb, with Muirhead Bone, and Francis Dodd was one of those selfless artists who though not rich themselves were prepared to offer the pictures of young artists for sale inside their own studios. I did not have to wait long before I received a characteristic note from him telling me that Lady Ottoline Morrell had bought it for the Contemporary Art Society for £100, which he hoped I did not mind! The news leaked out at the Slade and Tonks got wind of it, and was not at all pleased. He did not like his students going ahead of schedule, and warned me of the dangers of early success. In fact that was not to come my way, but this my first good sale enabled me to open an account at the Westminster Bank, High Street, Maidenhead, my father first showing me how to fill in a cheque. Fifty-four years later I was still following his instructions at the same branch of the same bank.

* * *

Life was moving along nicely for me now. I was a good figure draughtsman, and my painting began to come into the same line of controlled intention. Steer backed me as a landscape painter. The shadow of the Great War had not yet caught up on me, nor as far as I know on Stan either. His letter to Lamb about getting into the Bantams I have always regarded as not very serious. At the time of the resounding events of the retreat from Mons I shared the Summer Prize with T. Baxter. I liked his picture; I remember his technique was impressionistic with traces of Steer's influence. Mine was simply called 'Summer' painted from the Marsh Meadows in Cookham.

By the autumn other considerations began to disturb

me. Absentees from the classes became more and more obvious, and when a student entered the Life Room in the full regalia of a Seaforth Highlander I was properly shaken. Ugly characteristics began to emerge. I found standing a pint of beer to a returnee on crutches from the Western Front showed my preference for the role of the hero worshipper to that of the hero. For the time being I pushed on with my painting of 'Sashes Meadow', but the Slade was fading out before a series of events which moved me personally. Michaelis, a German we all liked and sympathized with, gave himself up to be interned after the sinking of the *Lusitania*; and Isaac Rosenberg, one of that sensitive and humorous batch of East End Jews and a poet, asked me one day if I thought he looked like a field-marshal, because he had been stopped by a recruiting sergeant. He responded to the call, and was killed almost at once.

It became obvious during the winter and early spring that trench warfare was going to put an end to any hope of a short war, and Stan and I had to make up our minds what we were going to do. I had no doubt in my own mind that my brother should go on painting. There were already five or six of his masterpieces leaning against the wall in our front bedroom. None the less he joined me on a training course of the St. John Ambulance Brigade and together we skirmished in Kidwell's Park under the command of Sergeant Major Baldwin. By now I knew I could not hold back any longer. I had no masterpieces leaning against any wall. I was still a student, but without a school. Thus the youngest member of a large family, I was the second son to go overseas.

There were no ceremonial farewells. I left unfinished an over life-size self-portrait '(Stoke Art Gallery) and, no longer concerned with 'Sashes Meadow', presented myself at Bristol to enlist in the R.A.M.C. initially for 'Home Service' to placate my mother. My selection of the R.A.M.C. was deliberate. Its record for courage is second to none in the British Army, but I chose it because being young for my years, and my imagination over stimulated as to what was happening on the Western Front I knew I could not use a bayonet, and that nothing in the nature of Sergeant O'Leary's V.C. would come my way, rather the firing squad for cowardice in the presence of the enemy.

For a period I worked at Bristol in the Beaufort Hospital at the top of Cannon Hill, but the falseness of my position in the Home Service when I was perfectly fit began to take toll of my feelings, and in spite of the fact that Stanley had followed me to Bristol, I volunteered for service abroad without discussing my plans with anyone. The night before I left, Stan and Budden, a violinist, took me to 'Carmen' at the Bristol Hippodrome. I believed then that I was heading for the Western Front and would be there in a few days. As I walked down the drive to leave for Aldershot, I caught sight of Stanley crossing the lawn carrying a bucket and brooms to clean out the Asylum Church. Out of these simple tasks came the inspiration for many of his designs at Burghclere.

Now came the first of a series of flukes which probably saved my life. The clerk at the Beaufort Hospital had marked my warrant 'Provisional Company' as though I had returned from the front via the hospital, when it should have been marked 'A Company'. I put it in my pocket without looking at it and produced it to an M.P. at Aldershot Station for directions. It meant nothing to me, nor to the M.P. but when I presented it to the Staff Sergeant in the Office of Provisional Company, he did show some surprise at the smartness of my appearance.

Sitting on the floor in the corner was a shabby shell shocked returnee from the front. None the less I was directed to a block in the married quarters, and proceeded down a whitewashed passage and up a flight of stone steps following the sound of voices. Entering the room which was thick with tobacco smoke I found a number of soldiers sitting on the floor playing a game called 'Banker' which I knew nothing about. I studied its rules till 'Lights Out' but did not, nor could not, join in because I had very little money.

For the first time I slept on the floor in close contact with a herd of men, and saw what they looked like in sleep, and heard the orchestrated grunts and gibberish that accompanied them in their strange dream journeyings to dawn and réveillé. And with réveillé the mistake in my warrant was exposed in all its nakedness. I had never been on the square in my life! All I could do now was to copy; and copy I did. A shrill whistle, and out the men rushed, I after them.

The yells, whistlings and trumpetings on that first parade were bewildering. The shout of 'markers' and 'markers steady' preceded a stampede in which we made a headlong rush at them, and by a process of shuffling our feet, and trying to see the chin of our next door neighbour but one, on our left, achieved the miracle of straight lines. There were many miracles as far as I was concerned during my fortnight at the Depot. It astonishes me now to think how without experience or fore-knowledge I managed to keep up with the Jones's, but the antics I indulged in on the square without detection or rebuke led me to realize the total separation of the drill book from the needs of the Western Front. I fell into other army ways too and learnt to swear like a trooper.

Fearful inoculations and stabbings presaged a move,

and very soon we were on orders for drafting. Kit inspection followed. Among the various trappings and oddments laid out on our blankets was a pith helmet, which created considerable speculation among us. Were we going to Mesopotamia, Egypt, India, Gallipoli, or further? We never guessed right.

On a lovely October morning we fell in as a unit, and with the band of the R.A.M.C. to lead us, and Lt.-Col. Smith at our head, we entrained for Southampton. I was young and romantic, but had no real feelings about anyone I was leaving behind. Still everyone else was saying fond goodbyes, and it would have been out of place not to do so too. As we travelled to Southampton we indulged in the sentiment of soldiers down the ages, writing letters to girl friends and relations, and 'posting' them, unstamped through the train window to be picked up by chance admirers. I believe they all reached their destinations.

4

Salonika

1915–1917

AT SOUTHAMPTON we boarded H.M.S. *Gloucester Castle.* I thought she looked very beautiful, painted with red crosses and lit up the whole length of her deck with green fairy lights. Getting away from the dockside was exciting, with little tugs dashing about at our stern seemingly unable to make up their minds. Sometimes they appeared in close conference, only to hurry away again with a sense of extreme urgency, until amidst sharp whistlings and some informative blasts on their sirens, the hawsers flopped into the sea, and we were in the fairway, heading down Southampton Water for the channel and the open sea.

As dusk and darkness approached, England without my knowing it was slipping away from me for four years. I was neither sick nor fearful as I picked my way with the rest to our bunks and hammocks between decks. But I was frightened, when we ran into the Bay of Biscay in one of its most tempestuous November moods. I really thought we would tip over. A leg-pulling member of the crew, gazing upwards towards the masthead, to cheer me said, 'Another degree and she will be over', but added, 'She won't'. We came out at the other side into lovely sunlight flecked with high cirrus clouds.

In these happier conditions, it was not long before

we were told to change into our drill suits. The relaxation of lying about on deck in the warm sun eased the occasional exercises and fatigues we had to do. Really it was more a luxury tour of today without the guide lecturers, for the general indifference of the troops to sightseeing was very noticeable. Only here and there an intellectual with binoculars slung from his shoulders, and reference books open, would spend his time consulting them or writing in his diary, while I, who had no feelings for that sort of thing, could only have entered, 'Saw the Rock of Gibraltar', though when a dark hog's back on our starboard came into view I guessed right that it was the magical 'Africa's Coral Strand' of hymn book fame. I noted too the strange and comic contours of Marseilles.

Looking back now I realize the extraordinary change that had come over my life. Suddenly I had been taken away from my training as an art student leaving behind my prize-winning drawings and pictures and yet I did not seem to worry over much. There had grown up some kind of amnesty about the fine art in its application to students in khaki. Bad drawings, bad paintings were now accepted. Even Tonks would be forgiving. However there are two kinds of artists, those who are born in love with art (Stan) and those who fall in love. With my brother, genius, 'the special inborn faculty of an individual', as the dictionary says, was apparent from the outset, strong enough to withstand the batterings of contending forces. Others not so powerfully protected might have become a prey to dual interests. Fortunately in my undeveloped and youthful state I escaped the dangers simply by not being aware of them.

We docked at Malta, which was so bright and brittle that I thought it would snap, to take on stores. Two hours out to sea we were paraded before the Adjutant to receive our ration of field envelopes and postcards, and with them our designation and destination. We were to be the twenty-eighth General Field Hospital, and our address would be Dudula, Monister Road, Salonika, British Mediterranean Expeditionary Force.

Relieved that we had escaped Gallipoli, we left the Greek Archipelago to the intellectuals, and turned to our correspondence, occasionally raising our heads to take a look as we approached Salonika. We were still a way off shore when we dropped anchor and were immediately surrounded by boatmen offering us everything in the world to buy except the money with which to buy it.

The town was just rousing itself. We picked out what we could see of it in the gap between a stationary stratum of cloud which hung mystically above, and the sea still as a millpond beneath. Clearly visible was the great white tower, and there were mosques and minarettes, singled out by their bells, and terraces of dark cyprus trees, unexpectedly emphasizing the white-washed effect of the town. On the other side of the bay rose a mountain. Some time later when we had established our hospital at Dudula, two or three of us decided to take an afternoon walk towards it to get a closer view. An officer asked us where we were going and when we told him replied, 'Well that mountain happens to be Olympus, and she is sixty miles away.'

The bustle, which we had been aware of from offshore, took positive shape, as we moved alongside. Turks, Bulgars, Montenegrans, even Albanians, supposedly our enemies, were all there to fight with the Greeks, our glorious allies, for the privilege of being official baggage carriers to the British Army. As carriers they used an unusual method of draping a sling from their foreheads down their backs to a little below their bottoms. We were only too quick to grasp this unique method of loading the beast of burden, as they had their backs to us and were unable to see what we were up to. Even mules would not have stood such treatment. As they staggered off towards the wagons you could see little of them except their feet, and their hands grasping at their loads.

As we marched through the square of the town in good order to move up to Dudula, seven miles away, we passed more shoe blacks congregated in one place than ever I saw in my life. One might have suspected that someone had tipped them off that we were there for no other purpose than to continue the spit and polish antics of Aldershot. In fact what we were really supposed to do was to keep the Turks, who were round the corner at Gallipoli, on tenterhooks. This intelligence came to us in a roundabout way, but theirs was of a higher order, for, having called in the Bulgars as replacements in order to contain us, the Turks packed their bags and crossed to Asia, while we thought we were still containing them. This offered us the mixed blessing of extended periods of inactivity. There was of course a certain amount of sickness, and we helped with the convoys toppling along up to our lines from the Monister Road, but so rare was it to come on a wounded soldier that, when we did, a crack went round that he had tripped over his own rifle. The mosquito was our chief enemy and he was bad enough.

I myself was detailed as servant to four officers. I suppose I must have made known to them my intention to be an artist after the war, but I had not yet formed the habit of drawing, and anyhow though the love was there and the conviction was there, I had not got any pencils. One of my officers, Lt. Piggin, quite innocently tried to give me a push in the right direction. Going into his tent to make his bed I found a little parcel wrapped up in brown paper for me, and on opening it found it contained a large box of water-colours with about thirty colours in it, each stamped with a design of some sort of Prince of Wales' feathers. They were of the kind usually given to children, so hard that I could hardly work them. I am sure I thanked him but I doubt if I thanked him enough, and still feel ashamed to think how little I responded. With Olympus in direct line of vision just outside his tent, what must he have felt that I took no notice? The answer I suppose is that I was then, and am still, the most English of artists. To those who knew, the flora must have been very interesting. I liked it, but did not feel sufficiently keen to break through the hard core of my paints to make any studies. Had I been a John Nash, I should have returned home with a sheaf of lovely drawings.

As it was I idly watched both men and women cutting the corn by hand not far from where we had pitched our hospital. They wore a strange kind of wooden glove with a wooden hook attached to it to sweep the corn on to the sickle. I also saw the flail still in use. Storks on one leg contemplated us from roof-tops in Dudula, and if we walked further on, we came to a rather swampish village called Topsin, where the houses hidden among trees, were on stilts, and dark inhabitants, some wearing tarbooshes, sitting on verandas, looked down on us through the deep foliage, apparently undisturbed by the chorus of frogs. The symphony of sounds coming up through the deep grass was always intriguing, and occasionally a grasshopper leapt into the air within the very shadows of Olympus qualifying for a 'gold' in the 'games'. But the friend above all that eased the absence of pets for us, was the tortoise. We used to attach string to them, plenty of it, and tie the other end to our tents. It was always easy for us to find them, no matter where they might have wandered. When we put our shirts out to air they would crawl onto them, some said to delouse them for us, but I was a little sceptical about their diligence, and the lighted match along the seams remained advisable.

There was little or no music except at our church parades, though I do remember a Welshman down in the valley playing the 'Men of Harlech' on a trumpet which remained an impressive experience. I regret now that I did not, like Stan, seize the opportunity to read more, but it was only later that my interest in that direction began to take shape; and I lagged so far behind in writing that even after the war, when I had been inveigled into going to St. Remy, the best I could do in a letter to my father was, 'Dear Pa I am sitting right on the banks of the surging Rhone'. Then I gave up! On the other hand I had brought off some beautiful drawings of French children.

Meanwhile, in Salonika 'the amnesty in art' continued and nothing seemed likely to change it for me. One afternoon, out for a stroll, I came on a piece of newspaper and, wondering what a Greek paper would be like, kicked it over to find myself gazing at a self-portrait of Henry Tonks. The effect on me of this coincidence can only be imagined. The artist in me also roused when the Corporal of the Officers' Mess asked me to do a drawing for the menu card for their Christmas dinner. I did so, and reproduced it eight times. I must confess it has always been a feature of my approach to my own work to love some of it very dearly; and I loved that little drawing. It is only six inches by three inches and I am looking at it as I write with the aid of a magnifying glass. I marvel at my

Tomato Soup

Fish

Mutton Cutlets

Green Peas

Roast Beef

Yorkshire Pudding Parsley Sauce

Plum Duff

Brandy Sauce

Sardines on Toast

Fruit

Coffee

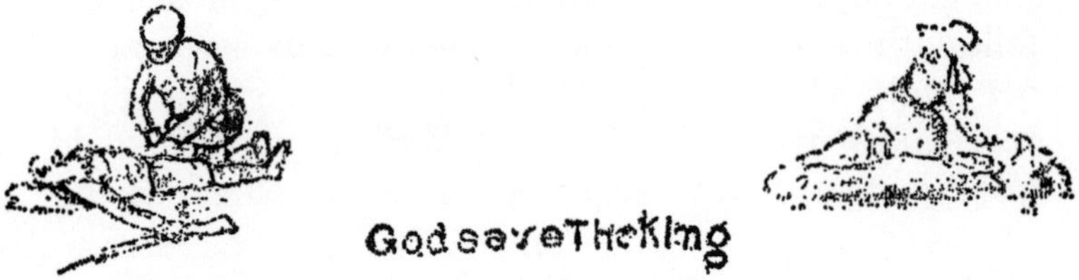

God save The King

eyesight then which enabled me to pack so much into it. Patriotism, humanity, an appeal to God to save the King, the floral emblems, fringed and ribbon-draped, of the United Kingdom, success to the Allies, a stretcher bearer attending to a wounded soldier in one corner, and a Sister doing the same at the opposite corner, all these are there, crowned with an overmantle of all the flags of the Allies held in position by the serpentine regimental badge of the R.A.M.C., and beneath it the scroll with the motto, 'In Arduis Fidelis', clearly visible. I like to regard this as my first one-man show, and what a success it was! When I came to clear the table the menus were all gone. Only my love of the sharp point of a pencil remained to me.

It was at this time that I received a letter from my sister Florence telling me that I had sold a little landscape at the New English Art Club. She was the pillar-box into which we fed our letters and she relayed their contents to each one of us so that we knew how we were all faring. I doubt if there were any other direct exchange of letters between us. Just once, shortly after I reached Salonika I received a letter from my father. He enclosed a formal instruction to my bank, printed out in his own hand, to transfer my assets to his account. This I signed, and returned with approval and sympathy. It was his only letter.

We saw so little of the war at Dudula that it was quite an event for us when the Serbian Army halted their retreat on the outskirts of Salonika. They looked and sounded warlike enough with the strange music that accompanied them. Some of them had their women-folk with them and one woman showed us a wound in her thigh. They did not stay long, only long enough to reorganize with French help, for before we could wander over to see them again, with colours flying though in French uniforms, they had melted through the mountain passes whence they had come, to the same strange music.

My part in epic events seemed slow to emerge. Most of the men I was now with had been at Gallipoli, some at Mons, whereas I could merely claim that I had reached Salonika by a fluke. So it was with some satisfaction that I found one sunny afternoon, when we were raided by Taubes trying to get a munition dump nearby, that others felt as frightened as I did. One man who had been on Gallipoli ran flat out like a hare, somersaulting down a ravine. The Taubes came again while I was making an officer's bed and, at the critical moment of impact when the bombs sounded as though they were coming straight at my head, I dived head first beneath a basketwork chair. The French tried to get them on target with their guns or to chase them in their planes, but these, like all planes at that time, could only climb spirally (the pilots used to wave to us as they came round each time on their way up) and the Taubes were well on their way back to Sofia before they could reach them.

The Zeppelin was much more frightening. To make matters worse we always got a signal when she had left Sofia. In the pitch darkness we would lie around outside our lines and notice the stars being eclipsed by her tracks. Our tactics at first were complete blackout but later they were changed, and the Zeppelin got trapped in a square of searchlights which caught her underbelly. We stood outside our tents looking down on the harbour and saw her, looking almost beautiful, lit up by tracer bullets and by shells from the gun-boats in the harbour. In the morning there lay the monster with her back broken on the mud flats at the estuary of the Varda. It was said that it was a shell from the *Arethusa* that brought the airship down and that it had glided gently to earth without loss of life, but the French claimed the victory, and later we were bombarded with French souvenirs in the shape of silk handkerchiefs printed with a picture of the Zeppelin and General Sarrail, and finished with a flourishing 'Vive la France'.

Living under canvas in wintry conditions meant that we kept very much to our tents when off duty. We lay around, talking, playing cards, and smoking 'Red Hussars' with a reckless indifference to our health. Court musicians were not allotted to the tents but they emerged. In our case it was a man called Briggs who sang 'The Volunteer Organist' for us, reviving in me, in acute form, my own musical aspirations. As time went on real talent emerged, and there were concerts and plays at which the goodwill of the patients always assured a highly appreciative audience.

Apart from kick-about football and boxing for those who wished, I was certainly in at the birth of 'bingo', christened 'housie housie'. It was not difficult to play provided one had familiarized oneself with the numbers on the cards, and in time I got to know that 'Kelly's eye' was number one, 'clickety-click' number sixty-six, and that 'Top of the house' was ninety. About this game there was some rarefied atmosphere of sanctity. Padres could play it without blushing. The explanation was that it was the only game of chance permitted by the Army Council. However their strictures made it so dull, if not positively silly, that few people wanted to play it, or indeed cared much whether they won or not as the winnings were also controlled. Its near neighbour, 'Crown and Anchor' did not suffer from sanctity nor the presence of padres, however strong their missionary instincts, for King's Rules and Regulations had laid it down that it was illegal, and Mounted

Military Police were authorized to spur their horses and charge straight at any group of players who showed up in their binoculars. I got mixed up in one of these games when we were spotted down a ravine. We fled, scooping up all the drachmas we could grab in the general shemozzle, and leaving the M.C. alone with nothing but his dice, to deal with the police.

5

Egypt

1917–1919

MONTHS passed and the pattern of life became increasingly restricted. For reasons of health Salonika was put out of bounds. Now only Dudula, Topsin, and a walk around the hospital lines were left to us, and I began to feel I needed a change. The responsibility of four Sam Browne belts, four pairs of boots and shaving water were not enough to sustain me for a whole world war, and I asked for a transfer.

Within twenty-four hours a friend named Edmonds and I were on our way. I had asked for a field ambulance, while Edmonds whose home was at Southampton had asked for a hospital ship hoping that there might be opportunities for getting home leave at intervals. When we reached Salonika however it was I, and not he, who was put on a pinnace waiting to transfer me to the hospital ship *Laetitia* soon to put to sea with me on board for nearly six months. For the second time my fate was decided by an error in my warrant. It was no use arguing with the port authorities or the harbour master. The last I saw of poor Edmonds, he was making his way to the Depot, still protesting.

I was greeted on board ship by the Sergeant Major, a very gentlemanly man who shook hands with me and handed me on to a 'two-ringer' nursing orderly, a sharp man, but reliable. My journey out on the *Gloucester*

Castle had given me a fair insight into hospital ships, and their way of life, and soon I was hard at work in one of the wards. These were between decks, except for the officers who were in the cabins on the main deck. The ward I worked in had seventy beds. There were nursing sisters as well as orderlies, and a sense of shared responsibility which I liked. In one of the corners of the ward was an odd-looking contraption, which proved to be the escape hatch for the patients. One of our responsibilities in an emergency was to send all our bed patients up to the boat deck by means of the hatch, but the occasion never arose.

During the many trips between Alexandria and Marseilles I saw many hundreds of beautiful pictures framed by the port holes as we sped along, but I never got down to naming them. However, once at Marseilles when we were tied up for some time while arrangements were being made to take on board a convoy of Indians returning home, I had an opportunity to attempt some drawing. I settled on a three-master tied up a little offshore astern of us. Once I got going with this I seemed sensibly to be recovering what I had learned and gained at the Slade. Drawing is not the same as swimming—once learnt, never forgotten, and the deeper the water the easier to float. It needs continuous practice all the year around even if you have to break the ice at times to get into it. On the other hand like swimming, one suddenly discovers oneself floating at ease. Drawing that ship did me a power of good.

The Corporal came and took a look at it one day and asked me if I would make a copy of a photograph of his wife. Under the circumstances, I threw all Tonks' strictures to the winds, and committed the maximum crime 'copying' that photograph with enormous care. Perhaps I had misjudged the Corporal for when he came into the mess to look at it he said he preferred the ship, and to please him, I gave him both.

We called at Malta, where we picked up mail and it was from one of my sisters' news letters that I gathered that Stanley had followed me to Salonika. We must have dipped stern flags (a routine drill at sea) as we passed one another. I think he may have planned to come to Salonika to be with me, but I had not the smallest inkling of it nor knew that if I had postponed my departure a week, we could have linked up again there. I feel it would have been strangely incongruous. He told me after the war that one evening sitting talking in his bivouac he heard a man's voice approaching exclaiming, 'If that's not old Gil Spencer I'll eat my hat' —it was poor disappointed Edmonds. Just as well that he did not know that only a day or so before, the *Laetitia* with me on board had sailed from Alexandria for Southampton.

Arrived at Southampton, we ran down the gangway, as soon as the taffrail was lifted, carrying letters and telegrams for the officers, in an atmosphere of 'Home is the Sailor' and goodwill. Our Corporal who hailed from Newcastle, was too far away to go home, but he managed, by fair means or foul, to get us some rail vouchers, and promised to send us telegrams giving us time to rejoin the ship before she sailed. By this means I was able to spend five days at home.

One could almost describe the peace of those late September days in Cookham as cruel. Peace was 'out of season' now. My contemporaries had vanished; and one went to tea rather sadly with their parents and sisters around the village. It is odd that I do not remember turning round Stanley's canvases which were leaning against the wall in the front bedroom just as he had left them, including 'Elizabeth and Zacharias', the 'Bed Picture', the unfinished 'Swan Upping', 'John Donne arriving in Heaven', and the 'Apple Gatherers'. I think I must have taken a look at my own unfinished works 'Sashes Meadow' and 'Self-portrait', and must have seen those of my life drawings which were strung up behind my little bedroom door.

At the end of my leave I went to see my sister Florence at Cambridge, where we were joined by my brother Sidney, who had just been commissioned to the Norfolk Regiment. We returned to London together, and I remember him asking some officers if they objected to my travelling first class with them; there was not room for me to salute them, but I certainly regarded this as a great concession.

Thanks to our Corporal, who was loyal to his undertaking, we were all safely back on board in time for sailing, and resumed our trips between Alexandria and Malta. On one of these, a patient died and was buried at sea. I was one of the bearers. Fortunately it was a beautiful day and the sea calm for the engines were stopped and we were adrift. To be in this situation aboard a twelve-thousand-ton ship was strangely impressive and a certain stiffness and solemnity unique in my experience was brought to the Service. The Captain read the Committal, then the Union Jack covering the heavily weighted body was removed, and with little ceremony, it was brusquely pushed into the sea. There was an awful splash followed by the sounding of the Last Post when everyone came to attention except the swooping gulls. Then we went back to our jobs, flags flew again from mastheads, and the compass resumed control.

It was soon after this that I asked for a shore job, and was posted to the R.A.M.C. Depot at Sidi Gaber, so that I came to know Alexandria better. I would gaze upon Alexandrians with big tummies, swaggering around in alpaca suits, black spectacles, and tarbushes, or visit the Casino overlooking the harbour. I wandered about with my hat slightly to the back of my head, and probably a cigarette in my mouth, and I well remember the sharp rap on my knuckles which I received in Mahommed Ali Square, swinging round to find myself confronted by the A.P.M. himself. He made me march past him, salute him, about turn, halt and salute him again before letting me go. Discipline was very strict in those days.

My stay at Sidi Gaber was short. I wanted to be on the retreating heels of the Turks just the other side of the Suez Canal in some kind of mobile unit. Stan was now active in this way in Salonika and though I was prepared to be left behind him in other ways, I had no intention to be left behind in this one. Consequently when my name appeared in orders to report to the 17th General Hospital at Victoria College, almost next door to Sidi Gaber at Sidi Bisch, I was most disappointed, until I found that I was to work in the dysentery compound. This was a real job. The patients were very ill indeed; and yet they were helpful and grateful. Once when I gave a patient a blanket bath, he blessed me for it.

I had nearly completed a year there, in which I only managed a drawing of one of the sisters, and a design for the theme 'Comedy, Tragedy' as a Drop Curtain for a play which was never performed, when a number of us were paraded and put on a train for Ismalia. On arrival, we loaded our baggage on to mule-drawn wagons, and foot-slogged behind them along the canal to Kantara, diverted by the sight of ships apparently gliding across the desert.

We found little at Kantara except some large tents, and store sheds amidst a general bustle of activity, suggestive of its future role as the base of the Palestine Campaign which was now starting in earnest. From there we made slow progress along the Mediterranean coast of the Sinai Desert as we transferred our baggage onto a rickety little narrow-gauge train, and constantly had to run back along the track and collect whatever was shaken off. But at last we came in sight of a few palm trees (Rumani), and a little way off nearer the coast saw swarms of Arabs, milling round like ants. We could not tell what they were doing, until the moment when a complete mess hut, capable of holding a couple of hundred people, rose shoulder high in the midst of them. To the accompaniment of some Rumani dirge it was carried bodily to a site nearer the sea where it linked up with the R.E. and ourselves to make the 36th Stationary Hospital. How we were ready for the first convoys from El Arish is a mystery to me. The Arabs were not able to understand us, or our ways, but they were an ever present help, and under intelligent direction, the miracle happened. Soon the hospital was full, and working efficiently—an oasis of another kind. Owing to its pleasant situation by the sea there was always a fringe of convalescents along the shore in their hospital 'blues', and red ties, relaxing and bathing, while we, when off-duty, could do the same.

I was sent to F.4 Ward where my responsibilities were as testing as they had been tragically simple at the 17th General Hospital. Now I often relieved the Staff Nurse for six-hour stretches, with only an occasional visit from the sister in charge of the section. There were many things to do besides general routine, both for the surgical cases, and severe 'medicals'. I remember that getting ready for treatments was like preparing a conjurer's table—two glasses, blotting paper, methylated spirit and a box of matches—and the trick worked! On one occasion I made a beautiful sandwich of castor oil between two layers of orange juice. As the patient swallowed it he eyed me with a deepening look of recognition. It was Teddy Spindler, a member of a well-known catering firm at Maidenhead.

Handing over to the Night Sister could be alarming; she knew what should have been done, and it was always with a sense of relief that I could look down my ward as she entered, and see all my patients 'settled' for the night. After 'housekeeping' with her for close on a year it is small wonder, when the time came, that I wrote her a farewell love letter, of the kind we posted out of the carriage windows when we left Aldershot. Wisely she did not reply.

It was at Rumani that I first saw Colonel Lawrence looking magnificent in a sheik's raiments mounted on a camel, but I wondered then, and still do, how right he was in his belief that we betrayed the Arabs, and how much it was the case that he had lost touch with reality behind the Turkish lines. Morale at that time was low, the Western Front in a state of murderous stalemate, Gallipoli lost, and the forces of Salonika fairly dubbed 'The Lost Army'. The sight to the ordinary 'Tommy' of a solitary camel corps racing flat out across the desert, looking for all the world like Washing Day, hardly seemed a solution to our troubles elsewhere.

It so happened that after we failed to hold Gaza, I found myself standing smartly to attention one day in F.4 Ward as Sir Archibald Murray sparkled past me on a tour of the hospital. Soon afterwards he was recalled, and Allenby arrived, backed by a vast array of artillery. The glories of Shepheard's Hotel in Cairo faded, and Headquarters were moved to El Arish, where Lawrence rightly feared that such a massing of guns would upset the Arab rising. But Allenby was in no mood to wait, neither as it turned out, were the Turks when they saw what was coming to them. As to our troops, captured at Kat el Armara, and at last released, I saw them looking like skeletons with beards, and it was clear that they had already waited long enough.

While I was at Rumani I was pleased to be invited to show some drawings at an exhibition at Port Said, but was rather put about by the arrival of James McBey, an official war artist, complete with servant, and a green armlet, to make some etchings of our hospital. In spite of this over-shadowing, I stuck to my pencils and drew one of the sisters who had teased me. It was horribly like her. I have it to this day, very much the worse for wear, but certainly one of my most successful likenesses.

In the end an order came that every fit man was to be trained for the Western Front. This was a bit of a bombshell. Bottomley took it up in *John Bull*, and questions were asked in Parliament as to the legality of transferring men to the infantry who had joined the R.A.M.C. through the St. John Ambulance. I was one of these, and had to fight for my transfer, but soon found myself on the way to Cairo and the infamous camp at Zeitoun for training.

Arriving there was a bewildering experience. The officers and N.C.O.s in charge were duty bound to tear the guts out of us instead of the enemy. Having reported, we were almost frog-marched to our tents and had hardly time to breathe before a surly corporal of the Leicesters burst in on us and introduced himself with the threatening words, 'I'm Corporal Clark, and by God you will know it'. From then on everything was at the double. If a whistle or bugle sounded, no matter what we were doing or where we were, we all started running. When the Corporal yelled 'Squad!

[confidently] Squad! [encouragingly] Balance Step on the right, Form [pause] Platoon!' we would 'balance step' like one man, or we would dive into trenches driving our bayonets clean through the stomach of a sack. At the time I lost all sense of fear of the bayonet. There must have been close on a thousand of us on the 'Square' looking in our drill uniforms from the distance like geometric shapes in the desert as we swerved this way and that to the yells of those N.C.O.s. The Sergeant Major ('Hindenburg' we called him) of the Grenadiers, moved among us like a London policeman in a city crowd. I grew to admire him very much. Occasionally he would raise his voice above the din, and, as we scrambled back into order, shout at some bewildered young officer who was trying his hand at drilling, 'No such bloody order in the drill book, sir'.

The training should have lasted only six weeks but time went on, and still I was there. Some of us were becoming so efficient, that we could have put 'Hindenburg' himself through his paces. I was picked out as 'Stick Orderly'—which was either a recognition of smartness, or plain Hell! Briefly I was 'runner' to Lt.-Col. Hubbard. I was his shadow for the whole day; wherever he went, I went, and indeed I had to run very fast. On the 'Square' he would thrust out his arm behind him with a scribbled instruction without looking to see if I were there, and I had to seize it, and race away to the orderly room, bringing back the reply at the double.

We had very little money, and not a lot of time, but my friend Jimmy Cowell and I decided that an excursion to see the Pyramids and Sphinx in the Padre's Party would be good value for ten piastres. Unfortunately all that happened when we got there was a fracas with two Arabs who had tried to cheat us, and whom we chased round the Sphinx. As for the Pyramids, I did not like them. A confirmed agnostic, I suffer a strong dislike for Paganism.

When at last I joined my regiment, the East Surreys at Kantara, nearly four months later, I discovered the reason for the delay was that there had been a fire in the Records Office in Alexandria, and in the conflagration I had virtually vanished. But for this, the third accident to my army papers, I would have been in France for the final push. Instead I had the pleasurable task of escorting 'Johnny Turk' as my prisoner, rather than having to shoot him.

The Turks were very amiable; some of them even had their womenfolk with them. One day I 'lost' about forty of them from my compound on a working party at a nearby dump. In fact I knew that they were behind some sacks collecting up a particular kind of cereal they much relished. When the Officer arrived and asked me where my prisoners were, not thinking that he knew how many I was supposed to be responsible for, I pointed in the direction of a little latrine, and said, 'In there, sir'. 'What, forty of them!' he exclaimed.

Armistice was in the air, and the rowdyism, and excitement that went with it kept bringing us out for patrol with bayonets fixed. When at last on November 11th, Armistice Day arrived I was on P.O.W. Guard at night. Verey lights, and rifles were being fired into the air all around, and the voices of the sentinels at their posts rang round the compound reaching the Guardroom only to start all over again with their reassuring message—in my case 'Number Five Post, and all's well'. Suddenly I noticed a German approaching the wire, and I adopted the correct 'On Guard' position. But it was only that he could not sleep, and hoped I might lower my voice!

After the Armistice the Battalion moved to

Alexandria for policing duties. By day we walked at ease about the city in pairs with our rifles slung, but after dark it was different. Then we moved about the city in posses with a sergeant in charge displaying proper military precision. As ten o'clock approached we moved in to clear the wazzas out. But we had had enough of military discipline, and were not interested in the niceties of peace-making. Thus when after three months we returned to Kantara, and got to know that Churchill had earmarked us to go on to Constantinople, we held a meeting, the purpose of which was to make our point of view felt, and to hasten demobilization. This was reported at home as a 'Mutiny' but it was enough for a General to address us informally on parade, and promise us that we would soon be going home, for us to give three lusty cheers for the King. He was a good king, and we knew it.

Not so long after I found myself once again crossing the Causeway at Cookham, and seeing the loved silhouette of the village. It was March 19th 1919, a date I had not dared think of when I left in May 1915. As I turned the handle of the front door I thought of my good fortune to be back again. Literally that was the only fortune I had, other than a Post Office Savings Book with my gratuity for £16 marked in it, and a letter from Lloyd George urging me to save!

6

Cookham to Garsington

1919–1925

I FOUND my father in his usual place reading, Mother, now confined to her bed, and Annie, with the help of our old servant Alice, looking after her. Except for an 'unlived in' feeling, home was much as I had left it. There might have been something of an anti-climax after the Armistice, but this was quickly dispelled when, in answer to my inquiry 'Where's Stan?' my father replied, 'He's up in Lambert's stables painting his picture'. This was right back to our pre-war habit of accepting the freedom of the village in our choice of studios. Cosy places in which to paint our pictures were more important than north lights.

Our greeting had little or nothing to indicate what had happened to us since we were last together at Cookham. When I told him I had come home via Taranta, he asked me whether I had noticed in the Mess Hut there a reproduction of the 'Lady feeding a fawn in the snow' a copy of which little print Mother had hung in our bedroom; and when I said I had seen it, he added 'Cosy'. I think I am right in saying that that was the only picture he ever saw on Italian soil. I should add that the word 'cosy' in our family vocabulary was strongly identified with a sense of home.

My circumstances after the war were different from Stan's, if not more difficult. In my time at the Slade before I joined the army, I had come to terms with my future, but not fully with my qualifications. After a few walks round the village and visits to friends and relations, I took my unfinished landscape 'Sashes Meadow' down to Odney bathing place, on the next fine days, to continue and finish it. My £16 would have been severely stretched if it had had to last for long without other resources, but I was given a student's grant of £90 which enabled me to live at home and pay my fees at the Slade.

The influence of the Slade before the war had been powerful, almost legendary. Those of us who survived and returned, found Tonks back in his place, but a little less aggressive. I remember his coming over to me and without sitting down, commenting that he only wanted to take a look at my drawing. I think he was looking for what I was hoping. It must have given him some encouragement, for when I took 'Sashes Meadow' to show him, he told me to leave it in his room, and asked how much I wanted for it. I said, '£15, sir'. Later I was sent for to find A. M. Daniels (Keeper of the National Gallery) alone in the room looking at it. When he asked me what I wanted for it I said, '£20, sir'. 'But Professor Tonks said you were asking £15.' 'I have changed my mind, sir.' 'Very well' he said, 'I will give you £30.' That was the only occasion as far as I can remember when my business acumen met with any success—even so it was not a lot of money.

I had another full year at the Slade, and it was perhaps the deliberate technique of a kindlier Henry Tonks that enabled me to recover something of what I had lost during the four years gap. Still I did not expect that on a visit to Cookham to see Stan's 'Travoys', Muirhead Bone and Henry Rushbury, who was keeper of the R. A. School, would give me a commission for a war picture as well. It was something of an act of faith on their part as I had little to show at the time. None the less I soon had my canvas lashed to a wall in a shed in the gravel pit up Cookham Rise, and began painting a hospital scene based on the 36th Stationary Hospital in Sinai which had plenty to interest me, though I sadly decided against a rather complicated scribbly recollection of a fire at the dump at Salonika at which I was present. I remember that drawing now, and wish I had tried to develop it, as it was full of ideas and feeling. There were gaps in the massive smoke clouds through which one got peeps of Salonika, the harbour and the distant shape of Olympus. We were running around collaring bales, some of them already alight on the offside as we rushed away with them, and there were mules and water wagons all muddled up with hosepipes and Greeks. But I was a slow worker, and perhaps it was as well the enemy did not go on trying to fire that ammunition dump so that I continued my drawing until the dump itself blew up!

P. G. Konody reviewed the War Pictures Exhibition in the *Observer* which it was my father's habit to read on Sundays and which I regularly collected for him from the station. On this occasion the newsagent, Mrs. Tidy, asked me if I would deliver the papers down in the village as the boy had not turned up. On my way across the moor I took a look at the paper, and came on the review in which after a few non-committal remarks, Konody likened the soldier perched on the end of his bed in my picture to the ventriloquist's 'Little Nipper'. It was a cruel introduction to my public, and the fact that it was I who now had to bring it to my father waiting at home and to the village in general made the lot of the prophet in his own country, the more bitter. But my father, whose appropriate comments and remarks were never lost on us, having read the notice, observed, 'Better be kicked than ignored'. This was a well-nigh perfect comment, and has held me in good stead as life has gone on. Also I could see how Konody came by his attractive piece of journalese. My qualifications had suffered through the war, and were not as yet equal to my feelings, but in painting the soldier perched timidly on the end of his bed, I had at least braved the fortress of truth. For straight from the battlefields, almost driven to the bathhouse, stripped of everything except themselves, their clothes tied up in bundles and stuffed into fumigators, those soldiers returned to the wards in their hospital blues like shorn lambs, seemingly almost apologetic.

Now began a way of life for me that was to remain—a battle royal for existence, yet with rewards of a priceless kind. No other profession contends with such methods and practices. By some means we have to find the right man in the right place at the right time, with the right amount of money. Or we have to have success at exhibitions where juries of artists, who have gone through the same mill in the past, decide our fate. In those days few were called, and fewer chosen, and it was only through exhibitions and the press that we got known at all, or through those more successful artists who brought us to the notice of their clients, and risked selling the bread out of their own mouths to help us.

There were then only a handful of dealers, who were great characters with strong ideas of their own, and a mysterious instinct which sent them scouting round select autumn exhibitions. A mention at the bottom of a press review might bring inquiring clients to these galleries, to sit in plush chairs head on one side, looking at pictures which the dealer produced from behind heavy curtains. It was in this way that one of William Marchant's famous green Goupil Gallery cheques found its way into my letter box. Wooing dealers was a tricky business. They took risks, not big risks, but risks nevertheless. They paid out monthly cheques though not large ones (mine was £12) and agreements were signed whereby one surrendered the whole of one's output to them which they sold, deducting 25 per cent for commission. A half of what remained then was given to the artist, and the balance set against these monthly advances. What was vital to an artist like me was to be able to return to the country to paint and draw there as I wished, otherwise these complexities meant little to me. I have always been a 'plain air' landscape painter, and apart from my 'windowscapes' have only once painted a landscape indoors.

My first one man show at the Goupil Gallery in 1923 was a success, and my press was on a national basis. With paintings and drawings together, there must have been 100 works on view. Unfortunately I no longer possess a copy of the catalogue, but reading Marchant's account to me (in beautiful copperplate writing) I see that he had sold eleven of my works for £158 and that No. 21 – (£25) had not yet been paid for. I also note that I had sold No. 33 'St. Remy, Provence' for £8, and it came to me in a roundabout way that it had been bought by Lawrence of Arabia. I already knew that he was a man of deep mystery, but though I was ready to respect his wish to hide his light under a bushel in Egypt, I was not prepared to hide his light under my bushel in England, and boasted of the sale.

The exhibition had been arranged to cope with the post-war years in which I seemed to have been doing everything but finding the right man in the right place. Later claims that my departure from Cookham had arisen as the result of a belief that I had not found the right girl in the right place, were certainly wrong when I went to live at Denning Road, Hampstead. I left Cookham and home in just the same way as anyone else might do who had to make their way in life, and learn to stand on their own feet, and I went to live in Hampstead so that I could link up with a number of friends, particularly the Carlines, whom Stan had got to know through the Slade. I make no bones about it that Hilda Carline attracted me. Her auburn hair against the lovely setting of the garden at Downshire Hill proved too much for me, but I had nothing to offer her which she could not gain from Stan. There was no rancour about this as far as I remember, and my painting and enjoyment were not seriously disturbed. The parties and 'whirlings around' as Mrs. Carline called them, continued as much a part of the life as ever. Occasionally Sidney and Dick togged up for a party in the West End, and I would stay with Mrs. Carline and Hilda and watch Hilda by the fire, but I did not lose my head, nor at that time my place in the family circle.

I might have hoped that she would change her mind when I was elected a member of the New English Art Club, which was something to be reckoned with in those days, but this was not so, and a letter from Orpen telling me that I had been elected a member of the International Society of Painters, Sculptors, and Gravers, began and ended there. Next a French journal of some sort wrote that 'the Spencers are good Liberals and were taught by their sister Annie'. Thus encouraged, when asked by my friend Christopher Hall if I would go to the South of France with him, I agreed.

On a fine summer evening a taxi called for me, and we were soon on our way to Waterloo, across the Channel and on to Paris. At the Gare de Lyon we found a first class couchette waiting us, and two Frenchmen with beards on the upper deck of our compartment, who grumbled fitfully all the way to Avignon. Christopher told me they reckoned we should have been up aloft. St. Remy was our destination, and I think I stayed there six weeks. From the point of view of my painting it was disastrous and clearly showed how right my intuition had been in preferring the prevailing winds from France to bring the message of the French Impressionists, over the Channel to us, rather than our going there to find them. I simply did not know what to look at, and the light dazzled me. The little scene of St. Remy was the only painting I brought back of any real consequence, and a dozen pencil drawings of heads, which showed clearly enough that I was overcoming the consequences of the war. I reached home alone after a series of flukes and desperate moments, such as when my luggage burst open at the Gare de Lyon and all my clothes scattered on the platform.

* * *

While I was in France it had been felt that with Stan's plans to marry Hilda now well advanced, it might cause me some unhappiness to return to Hampstead or was it rather the case that I was in the way? I have come to realize that Stan was much more affected by me than I had any idea of at the time. He said when he met me in the village he saw I was 'one of the chaps' and I suppose he determined never to let me get away with it, or to be left behind physically, whether as boys in foot-ball on the moor, or when I first joined up in 1915 and went to Bristol. When he followed me there I rather resented it, but had I known his feelings when I left, which he described to Henry Lamb, I might never have moved on. I see now that it was no accident that he followed me to Salonika (with what result!) and Hilda if she wished to marry Stanley could have played no surer card than when he told me, 'She says she likes me best'. I had punted her up from Cookham to Cornerways, the home of the Slessers, where Stan was staying, and after she had gone in to see him he came out and told me this. Twenty years later he wrote, 'It seems a pity I always felt a bit overshadowed by you when we were together'. But of course it was I who was overshadowed by him at Cookham, and now it seemed even Hampstead was not big enough for us both. Anyhow Stan told me that some friends of his whom he brought round to my room, had kindly suggested that I might be happier if I went to live with them at Reading. I thought about the idea idly, but there was no urgency about it.

Meanwhile there were many suppers at the 'Continental' with Henry Lamb and occasionally with Hartley which made good listening for me, especially Hartley's warning to Stan, 'Watch it! the little 'un's catching you up'. After a good hard day's work I could move around among paintings still on their easels, which are now regarded as masterpieces; or I could walk across the heath to the 'Vale of Health' Hotel to climb to the top to listen to Henry Lamb playing his piano. On one occasion he played the Diabelli Variations to Stan and me with his unfinished 'Strachey' leaning against the wall. Sometimes I did ten-mile walks with him in an attempt to ease the effect of his glassy eyed insomnia, against which he told me he had tried everything, and which knocked him off painting for days at times. With me, no sooner was my head on the pillow than I was asleep, to wake up next morning with my unfinished picture at the bottom of my bed, as was Stan's habit at home. No doubt it was Henry's jealousy of my good health which caused him to tell Stan behind a hedge in Dorset, with me in earshot on the other side, that I was too healthy to be an artist. Another time he wrote to him 'Gil's down here, putting in skies with one hand' which perfectly describes my happiness.

In fact life was very jolly, and I was much enjoying my painting, and my friends. I remember returning home one evening to find a note enclosing a cheque for £100 from Lord Henry Bentinck, who had called to see my painting of the 'Shepherds Amazed', and liked it.

It was in these circumstances, and mood that I received a letter from Stan's friends telling me that my room at Reading was ready for me. As far as I was concerned I had no wish to change my mode of life, but Spencers are at first too obliging and too angry too late, and for the next eighteen months I was cut off from all the friends and life that I so much enjoyed. By the end of that time, though my resources had become low, and my life heavily circumscribed, at least my painting had not suffered. The news of my mother's death came almost as a relief as it took me at once to Cookham, and while Father and Will examined with keen interest the wreaths placed on the piano and chairs, I took the opportunity to tell Percy, perhaps with recollections of his guardianship back in Brixton days, how depressed I felt, and how I longed to get away.

A visit to my sister in Cambridge filled a gap, but it was Sidney Carline who really opened a window for me. He had been appointed Ruskin Master of Drawing at Oxford and now invited me to join his staff. Once again I found myself caught up in a life full of companionship and interest. It was a serious school, but there was plenty of jollification between pupils and teachers. We were believed in, our demonstration drawings fondly kept, and we lapped up cheerfully what almost amounted to hero worship.

At Christmas, Austin and Vera Pool, whom I had got to know through the school where Vera was also on the staff (she was a good painter and had studied under Sickert) invited me to spend the vacation at their cottage at Chedworth. Thereafter I spent many vacations with them either at Chedworth or within two miles of it, not only because that was my usual walking range when looking for subjects but because Austin was a born countryman and seemed to have adopted the habits of Michaelmas hirelings by changing houses no less than four times. The family moved like farm labourers piling all their belongings into a wagon, and going first from Chedworth to the Mill House at Fosse Bridge, and then on to a small farm at Whittle. There was another move to Hailing, but it is to Whittle that I shall refer later, because it was there that they succeeded in bringing me to the notice of Kenneth Bell which led to my painting the murals at Holywell Manor. Meanwhile with them I revived my love of the country, helping Austin on jobs about the house and garden, or going long walks with Vera. On one of these she took me to visit 'Mr. Barton in the Fields', a small farmer whom she thought I should draw, as he had a good head, she said. When I had finished my drawing he asked for a dozen more! I explained this was not possible and that I was giving the drawing to Mrs. Pool, but I did make one copy for him for which he thanked me with eggs and port poured into a cow's horn made from one of his own cows. Recently in Christie's Catalogue, I read, beneath my name, the entry: 'The Master Farmer' 11 inches by 8 inches oil on paper (squared for picture).

By now I was holding one man shows at intervals at the Goupil Gallery, and later at the Leicester Galleries but though I enjoyed these exhibitions I was not at all brazen about them. I believed I had gained a footing with the goodly fellowship, and a place in the queue following the glorious company ahead, but of course there were anxious times still, and it was encouraging to find that the critics were pleased, particularly to read a fullsome review of my work by P. G. Konody remembering his first hurtful notice. Still more heartening would be a summons to the Gallery to meet an important buyer and to be whisked away in a chauffeur-driven Rolls to see his collection, shortly to include one of my own paintings. Once I came on Siegfried Sassoon wearing his old mackintosh, going round the show. He was a little shy and halting in his speech, and confessed he wanted to buy one but could not make up his mind between three of them. To try and help I made the gentlemanly suggestion that the middle-priced picture was the best one, and left him; later when I returned he was still there, and told me he had decided to buy all three.

It was at a Goupil Salon that I met Lady Ottoline Morrell again, whom I had just met at Cookham before the war. Thereafter if my reputation was not established, my domestic predicament was settled for Lady Ottoline said she would find me rooms at Garsington, and did so at 4 Blenheim Cottages. I was at once put on 'knock and enter' terms at the Manor, so that I often came into contact with interesting people, and also of course some very odd ones. As slowly my critical faculties got into their stride I was able to sort them out. For instance if I was surprised at the sudden escape through a little door out of the Red Room of Lytton Strachey, Walter Taylor and Siegfried Sassoon, it was only because I had not, as they had, recognized the voice of Lady Oxford in the hall. My brother Percy, whose offices were almost next door to her in Bedford Square, told me he had seen her calling to a milkman to fetch her a taxi, and such was her command, he did so.

At that time I had scarcely read any poetry, but did not find listening to W. B. Yeats difficult at all, easy in fact; all he needed was the shape of his listeners in his line of vision, though visionary he most certainly was. With the years I genuinely came to enjoy his poetry, but I got into trouble with him when Dick de la Mare (whose father, Walter, was a very different character from Yeats, full of kindly inquiring interest) suggested I should illustrate a short poem called 'Three Things' and my designs displeased Yeats very much. I did not mean to do more than clarify the facts of this mysterious little poem, by drawing the back view of a mother with her baby over her shoulder on the cover, and an illustration of a young man and girl standing on the shore with a wave lapping at their feet, which had washed up two little shells, and a fish bone. Presumably he felt I was oversimplifying the intended mysticism.

One evening at dinner Yeats fulminated against people who wrote to him for permission to set his poetry to music. He had a knack of conveying his intention to speak so that all were reduced to silence. In a bell-like voice he remarked, 'My wife tabulates all my letters, even those from angry musicians'. In the usual silence which followed these statements Julia Morrell, the daughter of the house, who was sitting next to me, said absentmindedly in an undertone that unfortunately could be overheard, 'I can't see anything in that'. Years later discussing Yeats' strictures on the conjunction of two art forms with Mr. Fox-Strangways,

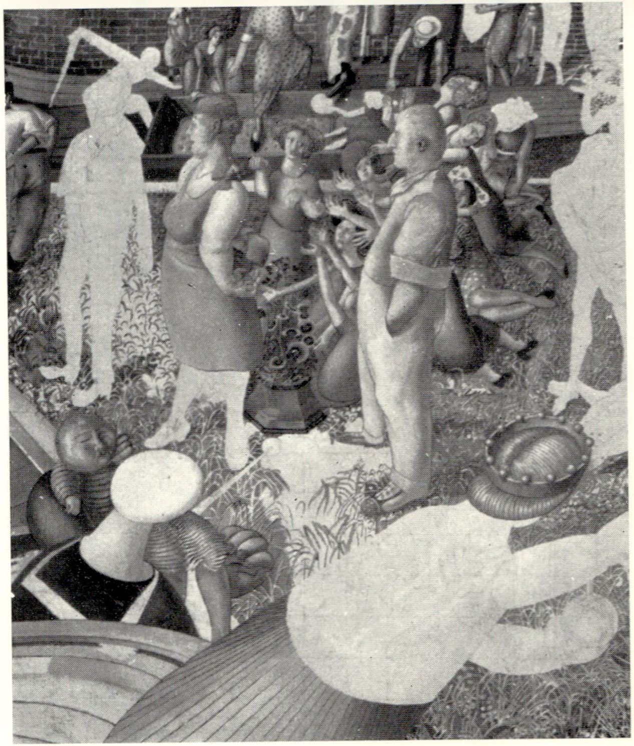

1b Detail from Stanley Spencer's
'Christ Preaching at Cookham' (1959)

1a The Miller (1921)

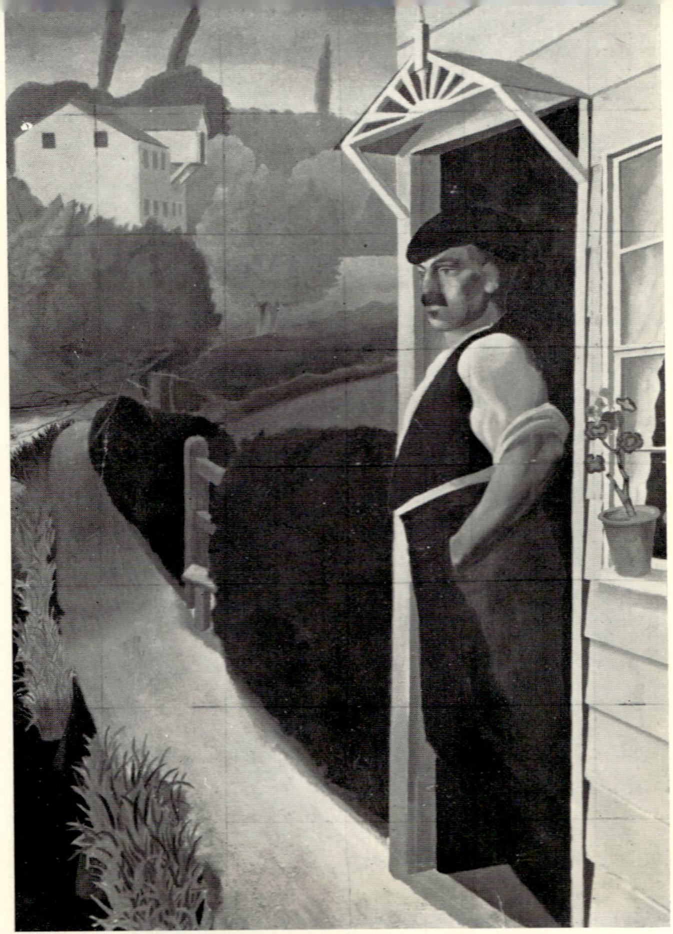

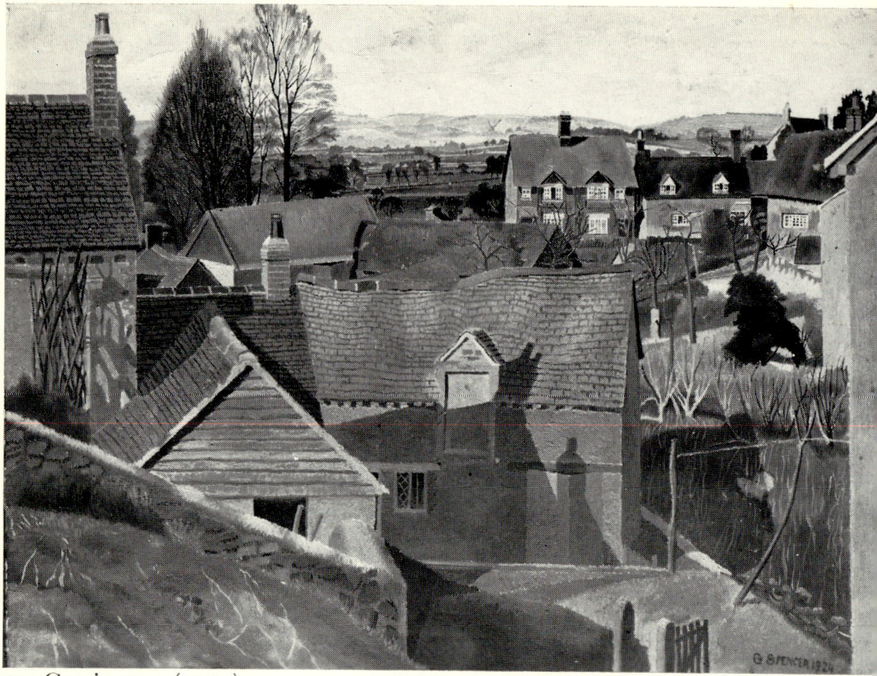

2a Garsington (1924)

2b Cotswold Farm (1931)

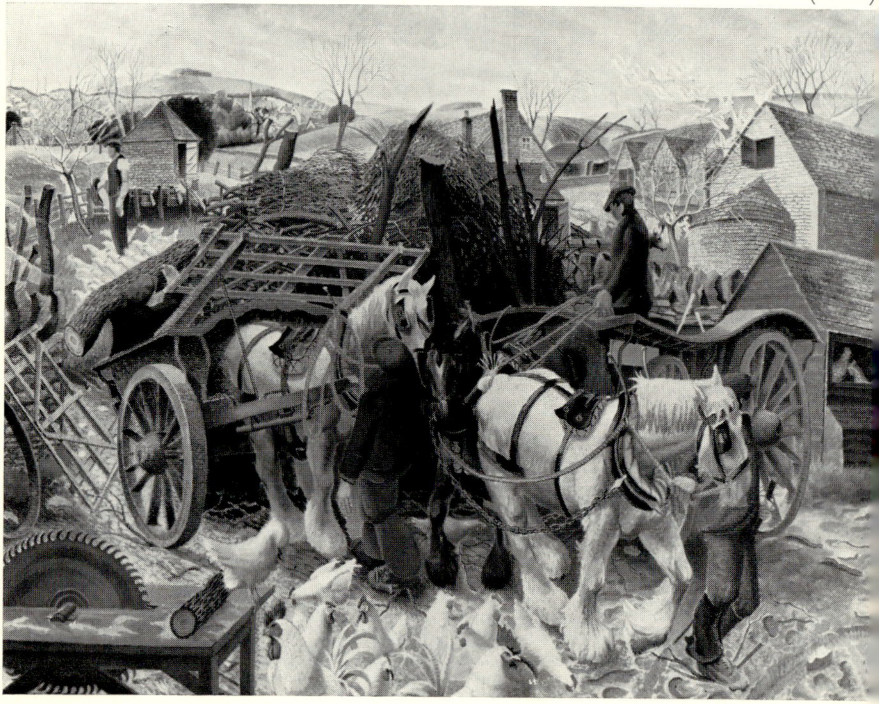

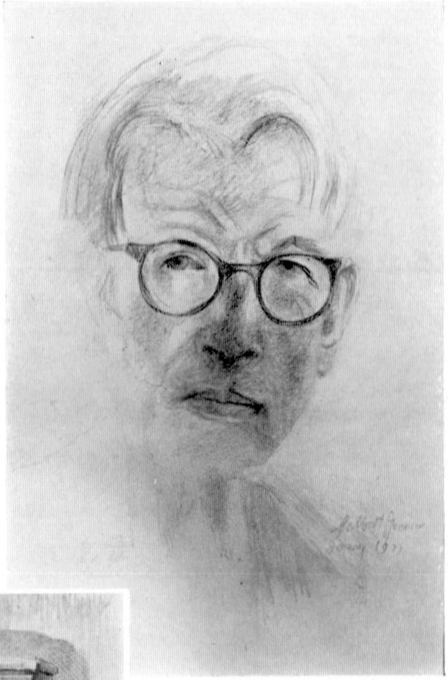

3a Gilbert Spencer (1970)
3b Ursula Making Curtains (1931)

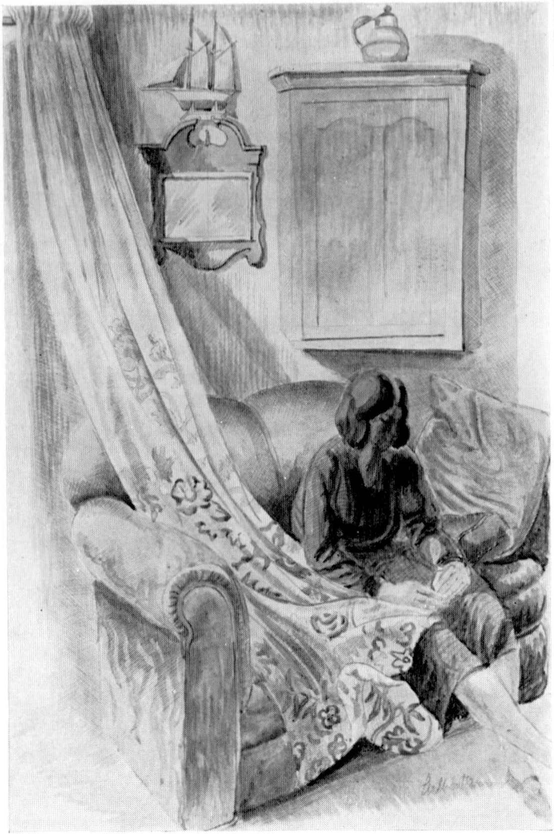

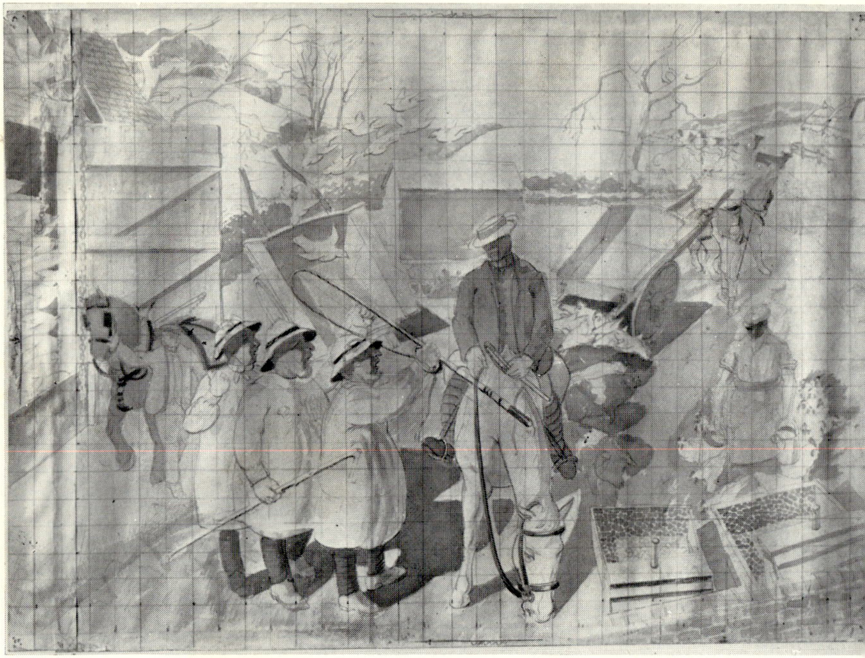

4a *above* The Beginning of an event in history: The Tolpuddle Martyrs (1931)
4b *below* Home Guard 'To make the fullest use of local conditions when adopting protective covering!' (1943)

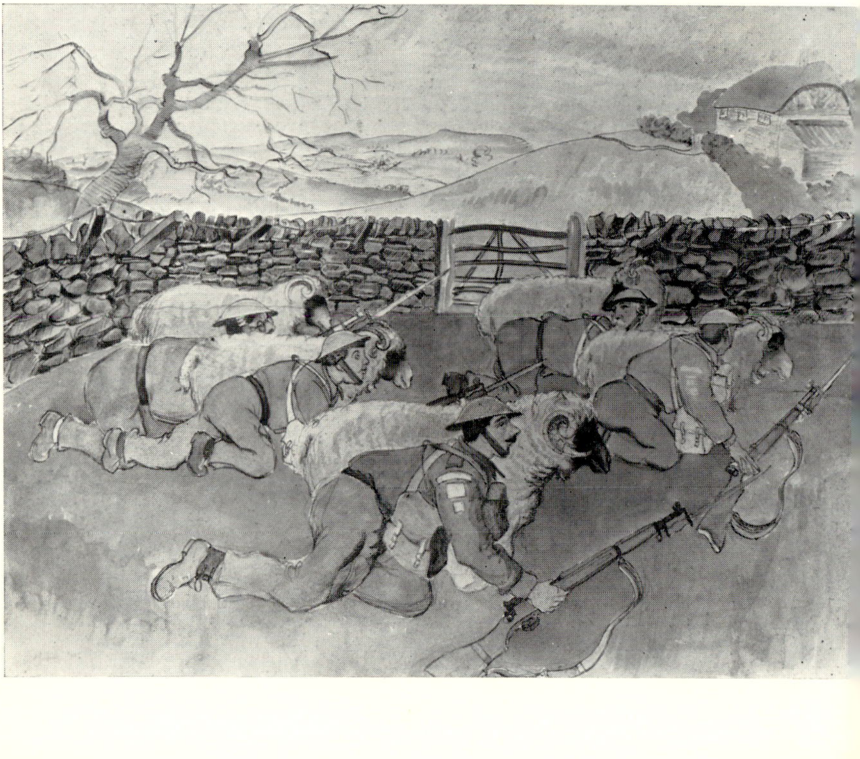

he went to his piano and played a few bars of Schubert's 'Who is Sylvia', and shut the lid without further comment.

It was remarkable how the Morrells succeeded in bringing together successfully so many people with contentious views and even a misfit like me among the Bloomsburys. Gertler summed up the atmosphere among us with D. H. Lawrence's avowal that he 'loved a good hater'. On those terms I should have got on well with them, and in fact I was amused to hear that Strachey said to Henry Lamb that I was like a breath of fresh air there. Stanley himself kept clear of Garsington but told me in a rather awed voice that 'people are saying it is wonderful the way you came through it, Gil', as though I had come through some ordeal of fire and water. My best protection was of course that I never sensed the risks, also that I lived in the village and enjoyed the close friendship of Philip Morrell's partner, Captain Woodruffe, and his family who lived just up above the Manor so that I was not dependent on the gatherings there for company.

It was the Bloomsbury's determination almost amounting to a conspiracy not to be caught on the wrong foot which made them difficult in mixed company. I remember the awkwardness which arose when a Rugger Blue, to whom Lady Ottoline had promised to be kind, arrived for tea. Her handling of the situation resulted in my finding myself almost at once with her and the visitor in affable conversation on the way to the croquet lawn, where she left us to play a game, returning hastily to the Red Room to explain away the 'hearty'. Another time Sydney Carline called to see me at my lodgings and was redirected to the Manor where Lady Ottoline took him straight out on to the lawn, and left him there while she found me. I was upset about this and quietly told her so. She was very tall and looked down at me with a characteristic 'Hm—yes! Hm—yes!' adding after a brief silence, 'All right dear Gil' graciously taking my point. She need have felt no anxiety about the reception of strangers by Edmund Blunden, Siegfried Sassoon or Richard Church whose sensibilities would put anyone at ease.

Among the visitors announced by Milly, the parlour-maid, was Mr. Augustine Birrell. I knew all about him from my father who had soaked me in Liberal tradition as a boy. His way of speaking in the House of Commons had brought a new word to the English language—'Birrelling'. Now, here he was, wearing one of those old-fashioned macintoshes with capes attached sitting in the Red Room, silent, excepting for occasional comments to Philip Morrell and Ottoline. He had a fine head to paint. A little behind him sat his invalid son from whom I believe he was never separated. There was no need for conversation between them. I have often felt what a challenge to a portrait painter to express this silent understanding between father and son which went deeper than any 'conversation piece'.

Mark Gertler was a regular visitor at the Morrells' and there used to be a great build up before he arrived but he was a very sick man at the time and would go straight to his room and remain aloof. I got to know him much better when I returned to Hampstead and we lived almost next door. At Garsington I never pretended to be on terms with him, or indeed with many of the weekend visitors. Personally I was happier with the quiet mid-week life of the Manor. In the winter evenings I might play duets with Julian or join Lady Ottoline in her boudoir where she would read to me, or just talk. At Christmas I went round the village with her carrying a large basket full of presents for the tenants, beautifully wrapped up and labelled with her florid initials, O.M. I remember entering the cottage of the head carter, Trinder, when he was having his dinner and feeling a little awkward before the truly enormous size of the helping on his plate. Not so Lady Ottoline, 'Well, Trinder, just having a little bit of lunch'. She was much liked in the village and this was indeed a feather in her already overcrowded hat, for they could be very critical in other directions particularly of the company that flocked to the Manor during the First World War and whom they regarded as conscientious objectors with no conscience. One has to admit that at times Lady Ottoline was as silly as some of her guests, but never, like Strachey, sinister. It was wretched how they exploited her hospitality when she was so good to them.

She was always good to me. I was grateful too when, later, Philip Morrell wrote the introduction to a publication by the Fleuron Press, in a series called 'British Artists of Today: Gilbert Spencer', in the form of a personal letter to me, which I reproduce below. It set the tone of what I wanted to convey in my painting then, and how I still like to feel about it.

'A Letter from a Friend'

> My dear Gilbert,
>
> You know how reluctant I am to undertake the task you set me, for I am not, and have never been, a professional critic. Still, if you insist, how can I refuse? It would be the basest ingratitude if I did. In old days, perhaps, I might have passed myself off as your 'patron' and then it would have been your business to write me some graceful letter of dedication: but now the tables are turned.

What is it, then, I ask myself, that makes me grateful to you for your work; what is it that I find in it so significant and refreshing? Well, first, that it is so obviously sincere; it seems somehow a true expression of yourself. Of that quality a friend, if he is worth anything, is the best of all judges. But long before I ever knew you your work attracted me, I liked it for its strength and directness, and for a certain unexpected subtlety which distinguishes it. I have never forgotten the shock of surprise and pleasure with which I first saw that admirable farm-scene of yours, 'The Seven Ages of Man'. Or take that scene which you did quite lately 'The Sheep-fold at Upper Farm'; what could be more delicate or more suggestive? And so one might continue talking of these country scenes, these village streets and farmhouses, that seem at first so absurdly familiar, so exactly and carefully are they rendered, but have in them as you show them to us, some subtle distinction of atmosphere, some magic of their own.

I have heard people compare you with your older brother Stanley, as if you were somehow under his influence and trying to follow in his footsteps. Hardly any suggestion could be more absurd. There is, no doubt a certain family resemblance, an intense sincerity, a kind of passion for accurate expression. But to us who know you both, how different you are: different in temperament and outlook, and in the whole intellectual 'make-up'! Let us enjoy you separately, each for himself.

For that is what I always come back to—

the strong character of your work. People say that it is very 'English' which is perhaps both a merit and a limitation, but at any rate it has a quality of its own, a character which gives it—side by side with the Johns, and the Lambs and the Gertlers and the Duncan Grants—its own proper place in English Art, and gives to us all, especially when we know it well, a continued pleasure.

Yours ever,

Philip Morrell

Garsington Manor. April 1926

7

Lawrence of Arabia at 'Clouds'

1924

WHEN I first saw Lawrence mounted on a camel in the Sinai Desert, resplendent in his sheik's raiment, I suppose I was impressed, but the enigma remains why his part in the Arab Revolt should be held to have had such significance by so many eminent people. John Buchan in *Memory Hold the Door* went so far as to suggest that Lawrence would have been the man to direct the defences of the country for the Second World War, and Bernard Shaw's fascination for 'Private Shaw' is well known. I was once shown a little book inscribed on the fly leaf 'from Public Shaw to Private Shaw'. Perhaps it was the aura of mystery with which Lawrence surrounded himself that had such an effect on people that their judgment forsook them and they lost their sense of proportion. I was to experience something of that mystery, and his strange way of life, but I cannot say in my case that it had great appeal.

While still at Garsington I was surprised to receive a letter as follows:

> Dear Mr. Spencer
>
> Colonel Lawrence has asked me to write to you and hopes you will be willing to make a drawing of Flying Officer Junor for the *Seven*

> *Pillars of Wisdom*. I enclose cheque for £5 on account.

The letter was signed T. E. Shaw, but the signature on the cheque was 'Ross'. When accepting I was aware that 'Shaw' and Lawrence were one and the same person, but who the third person in the trilogy was I then did not know. Later I discovered that Lawrence kept his bank account in the name of Ross.

The drawing was not a good one, and I did not send it, neither did I return the cheque, hoping for a further opportunity to try again; but unhappily Junor was killed in a flying accident.

It must have been a year later, when I was playing cricket with some farmer friends at Stourpane that a little thickset soldier came on to the field, and sat down by a hedge. I was batting at the time, and one of the fielders told me that he wanted to see me, but that I was to complete my innings first. As I was approaching him, I noticed he had placed his finger on his lips. This puzzled me, but when, after some hesitation he said 'Shaw' I jumped to his identity, and accepted what in any other man I would have regarded as an excessive anxiety regarding his privacy. There were only a few cows grazing nearby.

Nevertheless I was careful not to give my landlady any inkling as to whom she had in her little front parlour with me looking at my pictures. He asked me to go over to 'Clouds', his home, to paint a picture for him, but he seemed shy, and I cannot remember anything of our conversation, as one might expect, meeting him for the first time. It is his departure that comes more clearly to my mind. Having cocked his leg over the saddle of his motorbike, a 'Red Indian', he straddled it while adjusting his goggles and head-gear, and then revved his accelerator for a deafening moment or two, leaned over so low that he appeared to be looking under, rather than over, the handlebars, and vanished.

I followed up his invitation the following summer. I knew that Clouds was on the fringe of a great Aldershot depot, and expected I would be not unfamiliar with the kind of life that would be to hand there with its echoes of the war.

I found the cottage hidden away in a spinney, and reached by a road-track between high rhododendron bushes. It had the appearance of a keeper's cottage. There were two or three Tank Corps men on a patch of grass outside, and in response to my inquiry one of them shouted 'Shaw!', and he came down the little stairs to meet me as I entered the open door.

There was no reason for formalities of course, but almost at once an odd kind of formality crept in as he showed me round the house. This would have been more understandable if the house, and its arrangements had been normal. I was struck too by the slow tempo of Lawrence's manner compared to the motorbike incident.

We entered a sizeable room on our left and were greeted by a string of oaths from some soldiers who were plastering the ceiling. Some of it had collapsed on top of them as the result of people walking about above. Lawrence appeared not to notice, but quietly directed my attention to rows of shelves lining the walls, laden with delicious food and delicacies, and hoped I might find something to my liking to eat. Since I had had no food since breakfast, and it was now four o'clock, I could see plenty. Indeed I nearly lost my head on sight, with a 'Come on boys, get stuck into it!' But it was to be near midnight before I did so.

Lawrence next invited me to cross the passage to be

shown the bathroom. He turned the handle but without effect, so naturally I thought someone was bathing, but he put his shoulder to the door and pushed and I pushed too, till it burst open. There was nothing but dead wood inside. Lawrence explained that as the bath had not yet come they were using the room to dry the wood for the fire upstairs. There seemed to be a tree growing up through the floor holding up the floor of the room above.

On our way upstairs we ran into a soldier who wanted there and then to show me some drawings, jammed as we were on the staircase. They were not bad, and I said a few words of encouragement. But uneasiness was growing on me, and I sensed false values. For instance in the sitting-room a Company Sergeant Major sat with the poems of Laurence Binyon on his lap, but was he really reading them? Another soldier was said to be writing about sea voyages, but had only the Channel crossing in his experience. Lawrence squatted Arab fashion on his dais, correcting galley proofs of *The Seven Pillars of Wisdom* which coiled about him snake-like, and finally tailed off among endless dirty black cups and saucers. He said the washing up was left until there were no more clean cups. Then he called to the soldier who had shown me his drawings, 'Frost, put the "Jupiter" on for Spencer. He will like that.' I felt that the whole scene had been rehearsed in order to impress me. I tried to accept it all with a display of normality, but I felt strained and nervous being entertained in this embarrassing way.

At ten o'clock Lawrence rose, and started putting on his belt, saying, 'For obvious reasons we do not sleep here and have to get back to camp, but Frost has got a sleeping-out pass and will be all right with a sleeping bag'. Before he went he showed me my bedroom. There was nothing in it excepting a freshly made army bed with nice clean sheets which was comforting and reassuring after my odd reception. On the other hand there was a large space for a window, but no glass or window frame, and the ceiling was just lathes which Lawrence apparently had found particularly to his liking so that he had stopped the plasterers. I tried a little joke, but it was not very funny and anyhow as I learnt later Lawrence was completely devoid of any sense of humour. As we returned to the sitting-room he added adroitly, 'And usual offices—nil!'

All in all I began to wonder whether I could manage to last out long enough to paint a landscape. However after they had gone I felt a little more relaxed, lit a fire, and got the kettle going, and hoped that 'Frost', who knew the ropes better than I, would help to get some food. But I was discovering that Lawrence had some strange influence over his companions so that they became as enigmatic as himself. Clearly Frost had a highly charged belief in Lawrence's assertion that he was a suppressed artist, and felt he was cut out for something other than helping me to get a meal. He did in fact run off downstairs, but was back again in a moment with nothing in his hands, and put the 'Jupiter' on again with invocations to me to love it as he said he did, at the same time kneeling beside me and placing a beautiful edition of *Piero della Francesca* on my lap. I was conscious that he was looking more in my direction than at the pictures, and relieved when he moved away behind me to look at the stars through his binoculars, telling me excitedly that he could see the moons round Jupiter. On mature consideration I think he could not have meant this, but I was so weary and hungry, and bewildered by this excitable young man, I could believe anything. Eventually he took himself off for a walk with his binoculars, and was gone long enough for me to get a good supper together. He had calmed down by the time he returned but I was thankful to turn in to my comfortable bed, and leave him to his sleeping bag.

A couple of days later a lady and gentleman arrived who not only seemed very surprised to find me there, but in the course of conversation gave me the impression that it was their house. Holding to the strict secrecy of Lawrence's identity, I could say very little, but fortunately Lawrence himself appeared, and explained that this was his brother, Professor Lawrence, and rapidly detailed new arrangements for me. Apparently 'Spencer' was to have a bell tent in the woods, and even as he was telling us this, mumblings and grumblings could be heard outside as a gang of CB men, like ancient Egyptians in bondage, pulled and shoved my bell tent on a truck deep down into the wood, all among the flies and midges. I had had my last night at Clouds.

Settled into my new quarters I began my usual vigil, searching for a subject to paint, and looking to the southwest for the weather. But I was unhappy in that place, and almost preferred the camp at Aldershot to the bleakness of Bovington Heath. It was like being in the desert, and very difficult indeed to pin anything down. Also it was an uncomfortable area for my kind of painting with tanks prowling round. At last I settled on a tree which I thought or hoped, would interest me more as time went on, but to my consternation one of the tanks broke cover, and went clean over it. Fortunately it happened to be a sapling and obligingly sprang back to attention after it had been run over.

Gnats and flies visited me in my bell tent, but Lawrence himself never looked in to see how I was faring and I never got onto terms with him. I was disappointed that he did not take me to see Hardy who lived nearby, but he took me down to the barracks to show me my 'St. Remy' picture over his bed, which I appreciated and, he stood by looking on approvingly when I finally hung my new picture over the sitting-room mantelpiece at Clouds. I believe it is hanging there still. Certainly in August 1957 I had an indignant letter from Stanley who was just as irritated as I when our paintings were wrongly attributed, saying, 'The National Trust is talking nonsense. I wouldn't put it past them making ridiculous mistakes. I am sure it is a painting by you. You stayed with Lawrence and I remember you giving a brilliant description of what the visit was like.'

I had gone straight to Hampstead after escaping from Clouds before returning to Garsington, and I remember the relief of finding myself again in the Carline family circle with Stan and Hilda among the party. Of course I unburdened myself of my feelings after that strange experience, and Mrs. Carline told me that I must write it down. In a crude and ragged way I did so, but this, my first attempt to write, was lost or destroyed long ago. However it was a beginning. Since my wife's death my pen has become, like the piano, a friend to me, and I pick it up almost as gladly as my brushes.

8

Abingdon and Hampstead

1926–1930

WITH the Morrells' departure from Garsington to London a big change also overtook me. Stan had written some years earlier that it was time I took stock of myself; but I felt we had to cut our coats accord-to our cloth. I was not the compulsive artist that he was, and was happy involving myself in other doings, provided I was not starved of painting. This was as vital to me as to him up to a point. On the other hand my interest in the piano was not trivial, and meant more to me than to my brother.

Thus when Lady Ottoline suggested, shortly before they left, that I might be happier with a piano, no sooner were the words out of her mouth than I was off to Oxford where I found a Goetz for £50—which she paid for. For some years to come this piano acted like a barometer of my fortunes; in bad times it went into store, and in better times it came out again.

Like most young artists I spent much of my time in lodgings and bed-sitters, but I was home-loving and had no difficulty in making contact with people in this walk of life. They were poor, and so was I, with every reason to respect and enjoy them. My first move from Garsington was to Spring Road, Abingdon, but owing to lack of space and difficult stairs my piano went into store. Mr. and Mrs. Walters kept the house, and their son, and widowed daughter, whose husband went down with the *Black Prince*, lived with them. I always enjoyed the way Mrs. Walters replied to any inquiry of mine, 'I will ask Walters', not 'my husband', or 'Mr. Walters'. I was delighted to hear recently that they still had two empty sweet jars which I decorated with the Twelve Apostles, and gave them before I left.

I was not idle at Abingdon. One of the pictures I painted there simply called 'Abingdon' is now in Peter Pears' collection. Another, 'Abingdon Rainy Day', was one of those chosen by Siegfried Sassoon, and when I saw it again at my Retrospective Exhibition at Reading the design struck me afresh, so that after forty-seven years I should have liked to carry it further.

Unfortunately I contracted quinsy while at the Walters. Apples (baked) brought up to my room failed to keep the doctor away. He came, far from steady on his feet, and I gathered from his mumbled and indistinct speech that rather than attempting to lance the quinsy, he recommended gargling with port. I could no longer swallow, but suspected that he himself had had more experience with swallowing than gargling. Later I saw his funeral go past my window, and noted that there was not enough room on the hearse for the wreaths sent by his many patients, many of them poor.

When I was sufficiently recovered, a postcard to my friends, the Heaths, brought Mrs. Heath over with a blanket, and hot water bottle to take me to their home at Boar's Hill, where I was soon well enough to enjoy good cheer and company. I painted a portrait of Mrs. Heath which I have always regarded as one of my best. It had an authenticity and authority about it recognizable in certain portraits painted long ago which convince one that they were true likenesses.

I never returned to Abingdon as Sidney Carline, who was like a brother to me, suggested that we should share rooms together, and soon my piano was being removed from store into the parlour of the 'Plough' at Little Milton in Berkshire. We first noticed the inn as we walked through the village, and hopefully tapped on the door. It was opened to our surprise by a very dark skinned woman, who hesitated at our inquiry, and we were on our way again when she ran after us, and said she had asked her husband, Sergeant Major King, and they would take us in. We early discovered that we were in clover. Supper was excellent, and we nearly exploded when Mrs. King, with a glint of pleasure, asked us whether we had enjoyed the soup. Whatever other ingredients had gone into it, one at least must have come from the bar. Our bedroom was a bower of Maltese lace, and no article escaped it. In fact it was Malta that had brought Mr. and Mrs. King together. On the wall above my piano hung a photograph of the Sergeant Major and a number of soldiers stationed with the Royal Berkshire Regiment at Malta, in action at the 'Storming of Quebec'. My history was just strong enough not to be taken in by this device of superimposing.

My liking for the village had practical results for in due course one of Marchant's green envelopes was on the breakfast table containing a cheque, with a covering note to say that my large landscape of 'Little Milton' had been bought by the Belfast Art Gallery. A smaller painting of the village was bought by Sir Michael Sadleir, and there was another of nearby Stadhampton which had also been sold. Generally speaking I was in good working order, and was pleased to receive a letter from Bob Gathorne-Hardy commissioning me to illustrate the Ten Commandments. This sent me

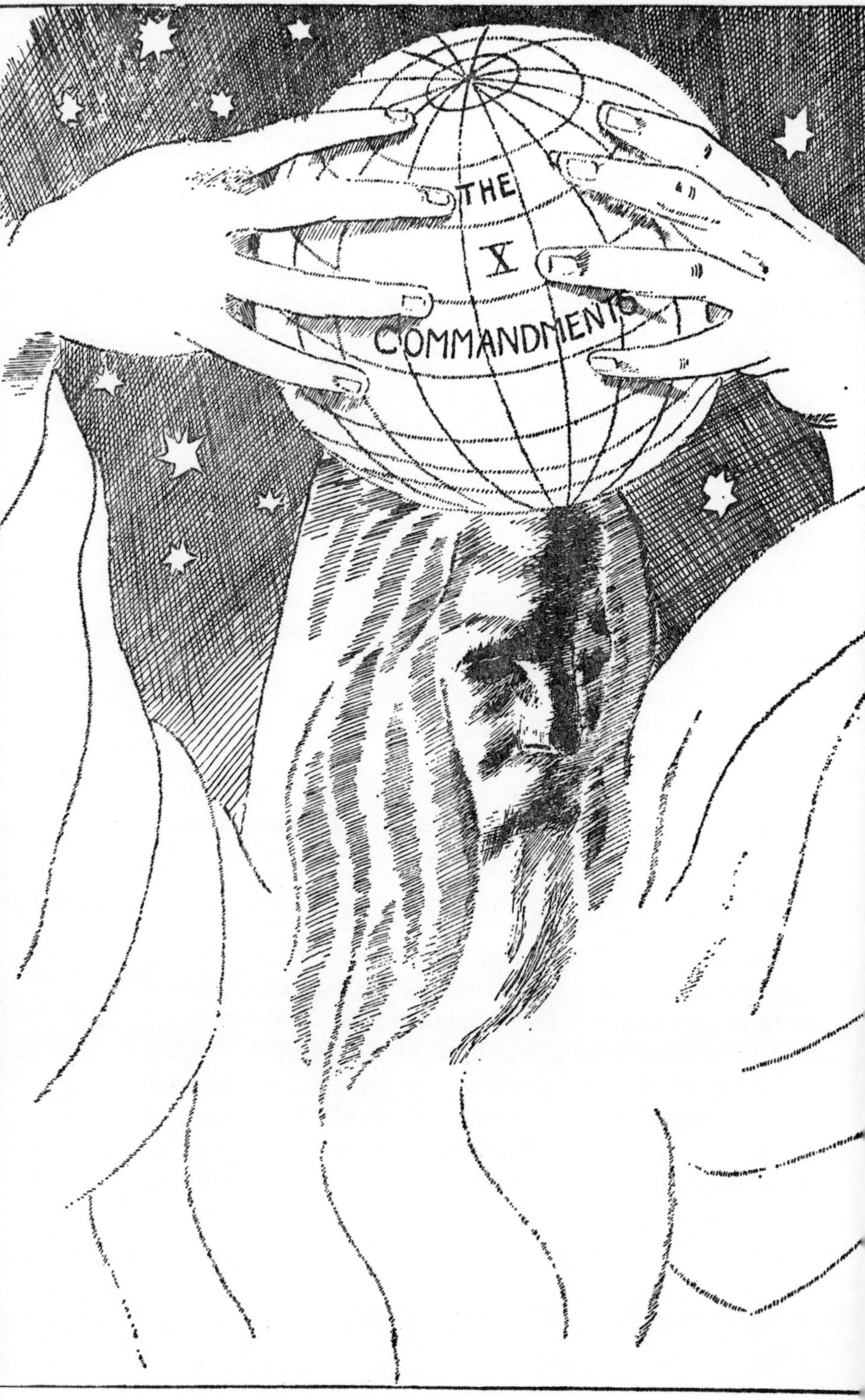
THE
X
COMMANDMENTS

straight upstairs all among the Maltese lace with drawing board, imperial sheets, pencils, pen and ink. As a trained draughtsman I could regard myself as something of an all-rounder, capable of work in a fairly wide field, and I put into these drawings all the orderliness and skill I could muster. It was just the kind of employment I was wanting, giving me a subject, scope, and discipline. I had to submit it for approval but there was not this time that tiresome question as to whether the drawing is like the sitter. Instead there could be discussion of a more interesting and varied kind. My brother's comment was 'Gil has found the Commandments all broken in the Bible'.

When Sidney returned home to Hampstead he invited me to go to live with him, and I was happy to find myself again in the heart of the Carline family. Their house on Downshire Hill was one of two semi-detached houses which held one another up at the corner of Keats Grove. It was a house of character, but not very safe. It had a balcony that looked, and was, too weak to stand on, and once a lion's head made of iron fell from the roof coping to the ground, but the family remained as unperturbed as usual and after looking it over carried it into the stable to take its place in a veritable museum of oddments.

The house was packed with furniture, but Mrs. Carline would have always found room for more. There was scarcely an inch of wall anywhere which was not taken up by one or another of Mr. Carline's pictures. One could look back to the time when the beauty of Mrs. Carline was hardly out of its teens, and his children could be seen all round growing up on his canvases. His kindliness, politeness, and love of family covered the walls.

The drawing-room, upstairs, was a place of debate

reinforced with tea and dripping cake till well after midnight. Sometimes Mrs. Carline would rouse up from her dozing crying, 'The bell! Dicky! Dicky! the bell!' and Dick would break away from the trays on which were spread his and Sidney's latest finds at the Cumberland Market to admit yet another caller to join in the banter, questioning the authenticity of some Easter Island effigies, Ming horses, Chinese dishes, or bits of Gobelin tapestry said only to need sending to the wash.

All this had been so much a part of my life before I went away that I settled down quickly and happily to paint in the stables, or in a corner of Sidney's studio across the road. There were old Hampstead houses to attract me outside, and on Sundays I worked in the garden painting 'St. John's Church' joined by members of the family on their return from the Third Church of Christ Scientist. For that picture a rich friend offered me £5 throwing in a drawing I had given him and adding the rider that he had just bought two of my brother's early pictures. I told him that he could keep my drawing, and that I would keep the picture. This was an early skirmish into the kind of embarrassments that I have learnt to carry off with a polite pretence of blindness which may in turn embarrass these self-styled clients more than they do me.

It was at this time I painted Mrs. Carline at her table in the drawing-room writing her children's stories. I hope that I got into my picture something of the associations of that room, and the atmosphere she created. She met life as it came to her squarely, almost harshly at times, where others might have given way. She was there on all her family's journeyings into the wilder and more dangerous parts of Eastern Europe, and such were her powers of assimilation that no sooner was the unpacking completed than she was out with her shopping bag as though she were back in Hampstead. There was a famous holiday to Zagreb on which Stanley went and where he painted two good pictures of a Turkish cemetery and a minaret. But it was Mrs. Carline who gained the coveted distinction of a one-man show in Paris—the only member of her family to do so.

A letter from Stan written as late on as 1942 reminds me of other paintings I completed in this period. He writes 'I was at Behrends about two months ago, and in that somewhat uncosy house, there over that high mantelpiece in the hall and in a somewhat darkish light was your boys playing with a football on Cookham Moor . . . Speaking of each other as worlds (I don't think I have overestimated our size *and* import) it seems to me that as your "Sermon on the Mount" is a good example of one of your hemispheres, so this Cookham Moor is a very fine if not the grandest example of your other hemisphere.'

This happy time came to a sad end with the death of Sidney Carline. I had been best man at his marriage to Gwen Harter only a few months before. As a painter he was studious, but not so gifted as his younger brother. Unquestionably his war pictures of aeroplanes which he flew himself with great distinction, were among his best, both interesting in design and humorous. His aircraft seemed to fly like kites, only remaining airborne by being tugged at with a piece of string from the ground!

On Sidney's death Downshire Hill was given up in favour of a smaller but equally remarkable house at 17 Pond Street. Somehow everything that had been in the old house fitted miraculously into the smaller one, including the huge Ghirlandio and the Lely, today joined by my picture of Mrs. Carline which has appropriately returned to preside over what is still the family home, the spirit of which she did so much to stimulate.

For myself I moved to a large unfurnished room in Denning Road, Hampstead. Furnishing was no problem. A friend ran up some chintz curtains, plain deal shelves made by me skirted the walls, and a large kitchen table, chair, and bed, soon to be followed by my piano from 'The Plough', completed it. But I was not always 'at home'. The need for country subjects to paint took me to Witchampton, Dorset, where I lodged with people called Duffett. Hand in hand with my enjoyment of country places has always gone my enjoyment of country people. Mrs. Duffett's brother died, and the news reaching Mr. Duffett one evening, he confided in me that having known his brother-in-law but slightly he would find it difficult to show his grief sufficiently to satisfy Mrs. Duffett. He also seemed to think that as it was already evening Mrs. Duffett herself might be too tired to give proper vent to her grief at that late hour, and decided that there was nothing like a good night's rest to produce the maximum emotional outburst. The next morning I was awake long before the appointed hour like one awaiting the gallows. I heard Mr. Duffett walking about, I heard him return from milking the cows. Had he told her? No, not yet. She was still chatting normally. At last after a terrible silence I seemed to see the black flag run up, and to hear the prison bell toll, and when I dared to go downstairs an hour later was almost relieved to find not a notice of execution pinned to the door, but Mrs. Duffett a throbbing mass of emotion on the sofa surrounded by neighbours proffering sympathy in the tangible form of black stockings and gloves. I got a special dispensation to leave the blind up in the room in which I was painting although it was situated 250 miles from where the death took place.

Shortly after I got back to London, I was surprised to receive a letter from Maurice Brown Ltd., who were producing 'Othello' at the Savoy. The cast printed at the top of the notepaper was dazzling with Paul Robeson in the title role, and Peggy Ashcroft as Desdemona. I was asked if I would undertake the decor and costumes, and was given an appointment with Miss Elsa van Folkenberg.

Completely in the dark as to how this had come about, I think it is astonishing now that I kept the appointment. How many flights of carpeted stairs I climbed to reach her I do not know, but of her beauty and humour there was no doubt. I frankly admit that on this first visit I had not seriously studied the play, and being in the process of building up a reputation as an essentially English landscape artist had never concerned myself with practical matters of stage craft and costume designing. However I returned to Hampstead with some sort of notion of what was involved and made a little stage set with curtains that worked with strings, which I played with for hours, and designed a costume for Othello. I chose a night scene imagining him in a white robe (a memory of the Middle East) moving about on a blacked out stage, and nothing but Orion's belt shining in the night sky. Miss Van Folkenberg pointed out in a motherly way that with a blacked out sky the audience would see nothing of Paul Robeson except as a white embryo floating around.

It was on this return visit with my unsuccessful designs that I learnt that it was my friend, Joyce Peters, who was in the cast with Margaret Barr's ballet who had suggested my name. Carried away by this well meant but misplaced trust I ordered an eight-foot canvas on which I intended to paint her in her ballet dress. But it was not to be. 'Othello' had a short run—in spite of Paul Robeson's giant striding about the stage, amidst draperies which dripped from the ceiling, typical of James Pryde whose designs had succeeded mine. I am not sure that my night scene would not have been more interesting. Still stage design was not for me, and I can see little connection between it and painting pictures. There is too much changing around and movement on the stage. Painters see their ideas from a fixed position so that at best I might have succeeded with some back cloths. As it was before I could start on the portrait of Joyce, she had left for the U.S.A., and I was left with an eight-foot canvas on which instead I painted 'A Cotswold Farm'.

This was a joy-in-doing kind of picture. True to my love of farm carts, I had to feel that everything in the picture worked. There was to be no cheating. It was an awkward moment which I imagined, but I knew that the experienced carters would avoid a collision, and that they were in fact just in the act of doing so.

'The Cotswold Farm' occupied my attention for about eighteen months with breaks for smaller pictures. It was essential that I should have it ready as the tour de force for an exhibition at the Goupil Gallery which was drawing near. It was the exception rather than the rule to sell these big works, but they stimulated interest and helped the sale of smaller pictures to which quite often I was more deeply attached. Of course there was a risk in giving up so much time to a large canvas, but it was one of the everyday hazards of painting among my contemporaries. Fortunately for me my own hazards were eased when in 1930 Will Rothenstein appointed me to the staff of the Royal College of Art.

My introduction there was a very happy one. As a

staff we were made up of the best possible mixture, that is professional artists who teach drawing and painting part time as we had done in the Ruskin School at Oxford. One of my pupils there had been Ursula Bradshaw. Her interest and enthusiasm, which were in advance of her gifts, had much impressed me when organizing the memorial exhibition of Sidney Carline at the Ashmolean. I wrote to thank her adding that if she would like I would come down to Bagley Wood to draw her father as a present.

The drawing took rather a long time, and is an interesting one. When it was finished Ursula showed it to Mr. Bradshaw, and told him that I wished to marry her. To his inquiry 'Can he support you?' she replied 'No!' We were lunching in Greek Street shortly after, discussing ways and means, when Ernest Rhys at another table overhearing our conversation came over to us as he was leaving, and gave us the copy of *The Ancient Mariner* which he was reading, writing in it 'You will if you will it'. We were married at Holy Trinity Prince Consort Road on December 31st 1930, with John Nash as best man.

The honeymoon was at Winsford, and almost on the first morning I showed a promising sense of responsibility. After taking a look at the weather, I got out my easel and canvas, and set off to paint. There was a sequel to this when I sold my picture 'Winsford' in Canada, for precisely the cost of the honeymoon.

9

London

1931–1934

WE STARTED married life in an upper flat in the home of Mr. A. H. Fox-Strangways in Lansdowne Crescent. Chesterton's had produced it for us from under the table when we were looking for somewhere to live, with a permit to view, and an introduction to Mr. Fox-Strangways. I asked him whether I could move my old Goetz in. 'All right', he said. 'Sound travels up.'

We grew to be very fond of him. Returning after an evening out we would pass his door where we knew there was a tread on the stairs that squeaked. This occasionally drew from him the much hoped for 'Is that you, Spencer?' and we would tap on his little brass knocker in the shape of a head of Shakespeare, and enter. He would be at the end of his large room, beneath his reading lamp, or lying on the floor wrestling with a difficult article, with Jock, his dog, asleep nearby.

One evening, in response to his call, we found him gazing into the corner of his room. He had bought a new carpet, and pointing to it said, 'It isn't square'. When I suggested with some hesitation that one couldn't really tell, he insisted 'But it does not fit! So I took a book, and laid it at the corner of the carpet, which showed it was plumb true, and said, 'As a matter of fact, it's your house which isn't square'. Defeated, he returned to his chair saying rather testily, 'Oh that's it, is it'.

It was said that Fox-Strangways' musical reviews were scholarly, but dull, and that Newman's reviews in the *Sunday Times* were more readable. However Mr. Strangways said that he wrote for the music, and that Newman wrote for himself. I remember he found it difficult to write about Elgar after his death. That seems stranger to me now than it did at the time. I now feel what a lovely string composer Elgar was, with his flowing line, and am surprised Foxy did not feel this too. In addition he had a great love for literature, and I much enjoyed listening to Ursula discussing poetry with him. To hear him read aloud Browning's 'Fra Fillipo Lippi' was splendid.

My first task now in the mornings was to go down and collect the letters which we read together in bed. Those were the days when letters were not pushed to one side. They were often very interesting, or even exciting. One I remember appeared to have been written on a piece of paper torn out of a notebook. It was from Miss Nellie Price, one of three sisters who lived in the Judge's lodgings in St. Giles, but always moved out for the Assizes. Nellie was the hard-working Secretary of the Art Club which organized exhibitions in the Turl during term, and my turn had come round. At first I thought that her scribbled note said; 'Sir Michael Sadleir will buy all!' but on re-reading, it turned out to be eight of them! Sir Montagu Pollock had also bought one. On the strength of this I gave Ursula her breakfast in bed.

After breakfast, I would go up to my studio which was just under the roof with a top light to which I was not accustomed, but there was plenty of room, and with the help of some gauze over the light I soon settled down to paint my big picture.

With friends near and far we were not lonely. There were plenty of parties and occasionally a theatre or concert. One day I read in *The Times* that Dolmetch was giving a recital of 'The Art of Fugue'—at the Old Queen's Hall, and I asked Mr. Fox-Strangways what he thought were my chances, not so much of my getting a seat but rather of my understanding it. He said I might try, and turning to the wall behind him, he pulled out a drawer like a kind of concertina and as he did so a number of programmes sprang to attention like soldiers, with tickets pinned to them like medals. One of these he tore off and handed to me, with his usual 'Off to bed'. It was for an eight-shilling stall at the Queen's Hall for the next evening. As I set out, he called after me to wait for him, and came down the stairs carrying a thick portfolio, so that Hugh Allen seeing us enter the foyer called out, 'Ah, Foxy, forgetting your notes!' But they were as much for my benefit as for his, for having seated ourselves he untied the portfolio, and counted out the parts into my lap, warning me like the schoolmaster he had been, that our editions were not the same, and therefore did not turn over on the same page.

Meanwhile in London our social life expanded, Lady Ottoline's 'Thursday afternoons' and Gertler's 'Thursday evenings' making an attractive double for us. Once we met J. B. Priestley and Ralph Hodgson together at Gertler's and as we left Priestley turned to Hodgson and said, 'We have had a good crack'. It had certainly been good listening for us, but Gertler himself was the most amusing of all. His stories were brilliantly told. I remember particularly a description of his going to a party and climbing the steps to the door, lifting the knocker, and then very, very quietly replacing it and the blissful sensation he had of returning home without having gone to the party, to find his studio as he had left it and his brushes waiting to be picked up.

These Thursday evenings were in the simple surroundings of Worsley Road, Hampstead, but when he moved to Haverstock Hill all was sadly changed. The drawing-room was cold and large, with heavy curtains and gold chairs, and instead of the old group of friends, there sat Herbert Read, whose book *Art Now* I found unreadable. I felt awkward, and made my 'get away' at the earliest moment. As Gertler showed me out of the door he said, 'I am not having any more "Thursdays" ' —not for you, he might have added.

That was the end of my relationship with Gertler, but even so I knew him much better than Stan ever did. Of course Stan used to talk about Gertler among others at the Slade when he came home in the evenings, and Gertler's fame was in no dispute, but he never came to Cookham and there was no correspondence between them. In any case Gertler wrote he would have nothing more to do with Stan after his rejection of Cézanne, and Stan's remark later when asked about Picasso, 'I haven't got past Piero della Francesca yet', clinched it. Tonks and Roger Fry also fell out over Cézanne, and Tonks's anger when Roger Fry included Stan's 'John Donne arriving in Heaven' in the first post impressionist exhibition contributed to Roger Fry's departure from the Slade.

In those early Cookham days Gertler's reputation far outstripped Stan, and the only parallel between the two was in their close ties with their homes. Gertler was as passionately devoted to his as Stan to Cookham and both were to give expression to these feelings with some astonishing pictures. But then Gertler, perhaps emulating Augustus John, started dressing the part of a famous artist. People would stand up in restaurants to see him as he came in with his black sombrero perched on the top of his black curls. But his gifts decreased as his affectations increased, and he began chasing false gods. I remember visiting his studio in the thirties and was shocked to find him rubbing grease over his pictures and flicking at them with a silk handkerchief, and then standing back affectedly to look at the result. Poor Mark, he had spend the war in a sanatorium, and ill health dogged him for the rest of his life. Unhappily his early gifts were not sustained and when he felt his fame was slipping, he grasped at the straws offered him by *Art Now*. I do not believe his tragic death was for domestic reasons, but because he could not bear falling behind.

* * *

At the end of my first year at the College, Rothenstein sent for me. He was sitting on the corner of his table with his short legs swinging off the ground. He asked me if I was happy. This might have been a Ministry of Education method of preparing to cut the ground away from under my feet. But Rothenstein was not such a one; he really wanted to know and was in touch with his teachers and students. Having given him my assurances, he looked at me quizzically before asking, 'You are not a martinet are you?' to which I replied, 'Not so far as I know, sir'. After a further pause he said, 'Very well, I wish you to accept the Professorship'.

Having kissed hands on my appointment I returned to Lansdowne Crescent to tell my wife the good news.

Will Rothenstein had a nice wit which at times he would turn on with lofty detachment. Once at lunch at Airlie Gardens, the conversation turning to music.

His daughter Rachel who was studying to become a singer, asked me whether I had a piano and I replied, 'Yes, an upright'. Rothy's instant remark was, 'As though a Spencer would have anything but an *upright* piano'. Another time when the Spencers came in for his comment was when he invited my brother in 1920 to go north to make drawings for Sir Michael Sadleir's scheme for twenty foot-high-panels in the town hall at Leeds, to be painted by six artists. Stan went to Leeds, but he never liked mixing with other artists 'on the job', and wrote withdrawing from the scheme adding that he objected to the 'principal'. Misspelt words were not uncommon with us, but Rothy replied, 'Dear young Spencer, if you are not ashamed to have written this letter, I am to have received it'. Happily all was soon healed, except that the Leeds scheme went the way of most municipal art ventures; the City Fathers, or 'philistines' as Stan called them, feeling themselves not sufficiently consulted, flatly refused permission.

My saddest experiences with Rothenstein was when he occasionally invited me to go and look at what he was trying to paint towards the end of his time at the College. I am cowardly at times. Perhaps my most difficult moment, since hypocrisy does not come easily to me, was when I spoke for the painting school at his farewell dinner. I remember finishing with 'In saying goodbye to the Principal of the Royal College of Art, we welcome the return of Will Rothenstein, the painter'.

As February 1932 drew near my studio became overloaded with paintings and drawings, presided over by 'A Cotswold Farm' for my next exhibition. It should not be thought that these exhibitions are for showmanship alone. Underlying them is the chance of seeing one's work together, and assessing it as a whole which is important for the painter as for his public. It is of course an anxious time for him when he takes down the shutters of his 'shop', maybe for a month, about once every three years. He should not do so more often.

I work slowly, and I had not got more than thirty paintings together at that time. With costs totalling £300 and dealer's commission 33⅓ per cent my net income from a show was only once over £500, and I could lose. With these figures it can be seen how necessary those part-time teaching posts were to artists of good reputation who had to maintain their independence.

It so happened that this exhibition at the Goupil Galleries was well received and brought a letter from Stan saying a little ruefully he was being 'brothered of'—brother of the painter of the farm pictures in Annie Slack's Shop (the talking centre of the village). 'The shop was full and Annie said "Oh Stanley, isn't this wonderful about Gilbert's show . . . *The Times* and *Morning Post* are full of it, and they say one big picture (A Cotswold Farm) ought to be bought for the Nation". Cookham rings with your fame . . . and I peep about . . . with my coat collar turned up! At the end of the general talk about your show my piddling little message, "Would you tell Mr. Shergold that I had not forgotten the photo of the drawing I did of him", fell utterly flat. I felt just like anyone who had come in and asked for . . . *Tit Bits*.'

My wife and I visited the exhibition on the last day, met a few friends, noted one or two more sales, and returned home. We little realized that night that the old Goupil had closed its doors for ever. It was my unhappy lot to be the last artist to exhibit his pictures there from a list of names so long and distinguished that it could have reached to the National Gallery round the corner, and in some instances had already gone inside. Sadly, as if waking from a lovely dream,

I now found myself attending a dignified meeting in a sombre atmosphere of reduced lights with Lord Howard de Walden in the Chair, and my exhibition, 'Cotswold Farm' and all, still on the walls. No one was interested in it now. Instead a few bowler-hatted gentlemen stood around with ledgers under their arms. I was there with Wilfred Evill, the solicitor and art-collector, whose portrait I was painting at the time, and he explained the purport of the business to me. John Nash too was there who first christened Mrs. Marchant 'Mother Duck' when she took over the galleries after her husband's death. She was a most courageous woman, adept at keeping our spirits up, with phrases such as 'an important buyer', and 'the critics are delighted'.

That corner of Lower Regent Street had meant so much to me, and many other artists. One entered the gallery down a long passage, dark and shabby, but not without honour. The walls were lacerated with nail holes. The nails had gone rusty many years ago, but some of the pictures they had held were now in public galleries, others indeed sold to 'important collectors', and for the rest there were always 'kind relations' or simply the dust of ages.

My brother was by now at Burghclere, pricking and painting his way like Michelangelo round his 'Sistine Chapel', moving as to the manner born among scaffolding, ladders, walls, workmen, and plans. We were no strangers to this sort of thing. It came to us naturally with childhood memories of Grandpa Spencer, the master builder. Certainly common sense and rationalism have to go a good half way to meet the hidden forces of one's natural gifts, or genius, as the case might be.

For myself with my show behind me, and my studio

empty, an invitation to stay with Vera and Austin Pool at Whittle was a welcome break for me, and a chance for Ursula to share my love of the life and beauty of that place. The view of the wolds by moonlight from the sitting-room window made one feel on top of the world. On one such evening when Austin was furiously writing and smoking, a Balliol friend of his, Kenneth Bell, arrived to stay and was introduced to us, but he was not exactly thrilled to meet us and spent his time talking to Austin. We sat apart with Vera, until the sound of hobnail boots coming from the scullery, and and the clatter of pails being filled with hot water from the copper was the signal for her to join the cowman on his way to the cowshed, and we watched them through the window walking down the yard to help a cow calving. When we went to bed Austin and Bell were still at it, smoking and talking.

The next morning I was aroused by Austin shouting to me to hurry up and come down. As I entered the dining-room I heard something that sounded like 'A Fizzer', and noticed that Bell was holding the photograph of 'A Cotswold Farm' in his hand which I had given to Vera. I was barely allowed any breakfast, and before Ursula had got down, had been rushed off by Kenneth Bell in his car towards Turville Heath. On the journey I learnt that we were on our way to the home of Conway Conway [Wertheimer], the Chairman of the Finance Committee responsible for the building of Holywell Manor, which was to be an annexe for Balliol College. Apparently Bell, on picking up the photograph of my picture, had decided there and then that I was the only artist to be entrusted to paint the Legend of Balliol on the walls of the new ante-room which was nearing completion.

We reached Turville, and were duly greeted by

Conway, but to every suggestion by Bell as to where the money for a mural was to come from, Conway, who was a lawyer, tapping his finger on the table, measured off in periods of imprisonment what would happen to him if he touched Balliol Trust Funds for such a project. At last Bell hit on an idea. Apparently there was a red-bearded bishop, who had left money to Balliol. He thought it would be perfectly regular to pay me from that fund if I gave the Bishop of Durham, who ambushed John of Balliol, a red beard! By this time Conway, who appeared to be mesmerized by Bell, pointing at me, inquired, 'Is he a Balliol man?' 'Balliol!' exclaimed Bell, in astonishment 'Borstal!'

Once away from the precincts of Conway's home, Bell turned quietly to me, and said confidently, 'Well, that's all right! All you have to do now is to get on with the drawings', and added, 'I have never had a more optimistic interview with Conway since the building started'. However since Bell's methods of circumventing obstacles appeared to me nothing short of a blatant fiddle, we returned next morning to Lansdowne Crescent not expecting that there would be any developments from Balliol, and I set to work on a picture which I took from a drawing I had made some years before while staying at Witchampton.

It had been the flower show day, and I had seen the exhibits being carried into the tent early that morning. Of course they did not arrive so conveniently together nor so perfectly arranged, but I saw in my mind's eye those lovely formal arrangements of vegetables and fruit awaiting the decision of the judges in the marquee, and I let my imagination run ahead, giving a formal twist to the vegetables in the barrow, so that they appeared outside the tent as they would later on inside it. I wanted the best of both worlds, the one I saw, and the other in my mind, and as my feelings strengthened about the picture, I ordered a near eight-foot canvas, and began to paint.

I had been working on it for some time, and had forgotten all about Bell's Balliol scheme, when on reading the morning's letters Ursula leapt out of bed as though she had been shot, crying, 'The Master of Balliol will be here in half an hour to see your paintings'.

I was thankful to have 'Witchampton Flower Show Day' sufficiently advanced to show Lindsey. Here was something I could talk about, describing how I came to paint it in that way—a totally different approach from that of the 'Cotswold Farm'. I enjoyed his visit but I did not believe anything would seriously come of it. Perhaps I could not escape a feeling that I was on the fringe of having five-hundred square feet of wall to cover at Holywell Manor, yet opportunities of the kind were very rare. After Burghclere my brother never had an opportunity to paint another mural, so what happened in my case, at Balliol after the Master's visit was nothing short of the miraculous. I was both surprised and dismayed to receive a letter inviting my wife and me to dine with the Fellows, dismayed because in spite of Bell's injunction 'to get on with the drawings' I had no work to show them. The brief reference in the records to the Legend of Balliol had inspired me to do no more than bite the end of my pencil. However they made me a most reasonable offer to undertake the work, and very soon, having let our flat furnished, we packed up and left for Oxford. We paid no farewells to Mr. Fox-Strangways, as we did not realize then that we would not be returning.

10

Balliol

1934–1936

THERE was still a great deal of work to be done at Holywell and the builders were still there which was to my liking. I had felt bogged down with the references to the Balliol legend in the 'Oxford University College Histories', but now, in congenial surroundings and company I was able to free myself from those complicated records. Later, after I had completed the murals, I made my own analysis of the legend, for the guidance of visitors at the Private View, the validity of which *The Times* accepted without question, and published on March 20th 1935, as follows:

> Foundation of Balliol.
> Mural Painting by Mr. Gilbert Spencer.

John Balliol wishing to possess lands belonging to the Bishop of Durham, ambushed him as he was crossing a ford. The Bishop complained to the King of England, and was released, John himself being arrested, was tied to a tree and thrashed. Dervorguilla, his wife, feeling that he had not done sufficient penance, gave money to sixteen poor scholars to come to Oxford.

Basing my ideas on this simple explanation, I now set up a trestle table in the room and settled down to work things out the way I wanted. I knew from the outset that I should start with the ambush, and finish with books and learning in a library. To give a more dramatic introduction I put the Bishop and four of his monks into an ox-drawn wagon, but this gave me no satisfaction, so I skipped over six centuries, and transferred them into one of the farm wagons I knew so well. Having turned my back on the past I hurried south to more homely pastures where I knew I could mix my own feelings and the events of the legend together more happily. For the ambush I first carried out a large cartoon of the Bishop being dragged away, missing his footing on the stepping stones across the stream, his vestments caught up and swirling around him. It was full of possibilities and exciting patterns, but it would not have filled the space sufficiently, and so I finally abandoned it. I was not impressed by John Balliol; I felt him to be a mean character, and painted him over the door in half an hour. However he became helpful to me escaping on horseback, with the Tipstaff scaling the wall to cut him off. Soon his hat and coat could be seen hanging on the wall and this led on nicely to him being stripped to the waist and tied to a tree.

My work at Lansdowne Crescent had got rather stuck but it was going well now. Probably it was because I was now 'on the job' and that men were around with their comments. I completed the scaled drawings and paintings which I used throughout without trouble, and had them squared up and drawn on the wall in good time, and in good order. Those preliminary squares were evocative and the essence of excitements to come. Stan naturally squared all his work at Burghclere, unlike McEvoy who, it is said, sold a drawing of a head to a client and explained he ruled squares over it because the Old Masters did!

My time at Holywell overlapped Stan's time at Burghclere and on one or two occasions I went over to see how he was getting on. I remember a visit when he was working on the altar piece of the 'Resurrection of the Soldiers', and we looked together at the soldier enmeshed in coils of barbed wire from head to foot, while another soldier with outstretched arm was cutting him clear. Stan standing just behind me said, 'You remember, Gil, we were laying barbed wire between the lines, and as that man ran along with it carrying it above his head, a strut broke, and it all uncoiled, and came on top of him like that'. It is impossible to convey in words his excitement, his gestures and way of raising his forefinger horizontally to his lips, and his glee at this 'hand out' to him for an idea.

On the same occasion he pointed out to me the blown up limber with the driver resting between the two mules, and told me he had seen one hit by a shell. I was impressed by the orderliness and beauty of the design, and wonder now whether that orderliness came to him from the memory that those wagons arrived in Salonika in sections, and were laid out on the ground and assembled from blueprints. The soldier lying, examining his cross, might well have been an engineer examining the plan. Stan must have seen this happening repeatedly and so brought it and the shell incident together so impressively.

Fortunately I was not overawed by these visits to Burghclere, but would return to my own walls at Balliol, and settle down to them again, in my own way, pleased to be sharing something of his experience. I too was interested in design and composition, and welcomed an agricultural setting because of the patterns that naturally appear round farms. How a Bishop's lawn sleeves and mitre could be justified in those surroundings, and out in that weather, did not worry me. An ecclesiastical setting would have left me cold, and only at the very end did I introduce through the windows of the library, a view of St. Mary's.

At no time did I feel out of place at Balliol, though I wonder if on the first occasion of my dining at high table, Bell had manipulated the seating arrangements so that I should not be nervous. My kindly neighbour told me that when Fridays came round he put on a cap, and went to London and bought the 'Pink Un'. Puzzled about him, I asked Bell later what his subject was. It turned out he was the College Bursar, Colonel Duke, a most beloved character, and a particular friend to me. Throughout the whole time I was working in Oxford he repeatedly received salvoes in the form of bills fired from across the road by Alden's picture shop, which I regularly visited in my blue overalls, and left again in high spirits, with my arms full of lovely materials, calling back to the kindly Mr. Grimsby 'Send the bill to Balliol!'

My first introduction to mural painting had been at Hampstead at the Vale of Health Hotel. Stan had finished the Cookham Church 'Resurrection', and to fill in the time while waiting for the chapel at Burghclere to be ready, he painted the first panel of the orderly scrubbing the floor. Compared with the 'Resurrection' with its wealth of detail and colour, this painting did not look very good to me at the time. Indeed, it would have been hard to foresee that it was the start of such a journey, but with the experience I gained at Holywell, I can understand now how that was. Going round four walls is a slow and a compelling experience, and one must be patient waiting for the cumulative effect. At the beginning one is naturally tentative, but as the work proceeds, egged on by new excitements, one may find oneself in trouble, if one works too fast. Then it may be a case of fetching the workmen back, and getting back to the bare bricks.

My feelings were mixed as I worked, loving as a painter two extremes of art: the flat art of the primitives, and that of the French impressionists. The flat art is what I wanted here, introduced to me through Gowans and Grays 'Old Master Series'. The reproductions were not coloured, just tonal, but they were most impressive and I think they played a part in the rich simple palette of Stan's early paintings.

We had many friends in Oxford, and saw much of Joyce and Gerty Cary whose son, Tristram. had been page at our wedding. Joyce used often to come round to watch me at work in Holywell. He liked the roosting chickens who had a good view of the thrashing of John Balliol, and said they were in the stalls—I thought, in the Gods! He also told Mrs. Lindsey when she came to see what I was doing that Balliol was being 'put on the map', by me, for which I thought he might be put 'on the mat'. I had a great respect for the Master's wife. She was passionately sincere, even though she was as often wrong as right. When she saw my painting of the Bishop she spun round, in a state of high tension, exclaiming, 'If only you had seen Bishop Gore'. In fact I had met him in the Garsington days, and should have liked to have known him better, but I kept very quiet about this, and went on with my red beard.

Any hostility to my painting the murals gradually faded. Duncan MacGregor told me frankly when I was made a life member of the S.C.R. that he had been strongly opposed to the idea of the murals in the beginning, but after a few visits to me at Holywell, he took on the special qualities of the true convert, not only praising my work there, but extending this to a form of head hunting. Ursula and I would return to our room to find pieces of paper pinned to the soft furnishings informing me that yet another fellow don or distinguished professor had been button-holed to sit for me. By these means I collected an interesting clientéle.

One successful drawing, commissioned through Duncan, was of Lady Fulton who was at the time Gilbert Murray's secretary. But I failed in my drawing of the Master, though I attach some of the blame for this to him. It was not a question of making a little conversation to counter sleepiness—quite the reverse. The 'sitter' got a pencil and pad, and started drawing something on the mantelpiece!

There was another sitter who did not come through Duncan but introduced himself by letter. He explained that he was coming to Oxford for the Assizes, and would be staying at the Judge's Lodgings where I could draw him at 9 a.m. This was Mr. Justice Finnemore. All the time I was drawing him he gave me the impression of sadness. His mind, and, to a lesser degree his mouth, never stopped working. Later he told me he feared that he had got to send a man to prison which would disqualify him from returning to his profession, and I felt he was reviewing the case in search of a lighter sentence. He ran boys' clubs in the East End, and assured me that it was wrong to point to any social explanation for crime. Some very bad cases, he told me, had excellent homes.

So many and varied conditions go into portraiture that I have never achieved mastery of it, nor can be certain of getting a likeness or giving the right impression. Henry Lamb referred to 'finding the thing that matters'. I am not temperamentally suited to the strain, and dread the moment when I know that I will have to turn my drawing round and show the result.

However there have been plenty of drawings which I have not minded turning round at all. Once my brother said of one of his figures at Burghclere, 'Only Titian could have painted that', and of a drawing I did called 'A Day in Bed' of my daughter Gillian, I felt I would not have minded showing it to Rubens. Taking them all in all I have had a reasonable number of successes, including Professor Galbraith, F. B. Wilson, Henry Whitehead, Sir James Robertson, Sir Robert Birley, and Sir Geoffrey Keynes. I failed hopelessly with Sir William Bragg, and redeemed a bad drawing of John Nash many years later staying with Hilda Harrison. I was struggling with it when Mr. Asquith called, and sat down to watch me. He was very respectful towards the artist, and full of trust. We all went to Stratford Old Theatre later to see 'Hamlet', and I sat next to him. I have heard him called the last of the 'Gentlemen' Prime Ministers.

Towards the end of our time in Oxford, Ursula and I had our eyes on the progress of the walls, against the clock. She had had reason to call on our friend and neighbour Dr. Raymond Greene who had confirmed her in her suspicions. So that she should take life quietly, lunches were brought round to Holywell on wheels from Hall, and teas, with anchovy toast were shared with our friends. It was cosy in the evenings in the twilight, but there were times by day when I could have wished a permanent twilight over Holywell. I had completed the whipping of John of Balliol but I was most unhappy with Devorguilla. In the end I used a drawing for her I had once made of Desdemona. I got on better with the scholars as they prepared to leave for home with odd cricket bats and tennis racquets among their luggage, and again in the next panel, as they first sighted Oxford. They had their arms raised in joy in contrast to the unhappy monks, and the weary horse, its head drooping with exhaustion nosing the grass, where the Oxfordshire fritillary grew. At last there were the scholars resting and reading in the library, having reached the end of their journey, as I had come to the end of mine.

There was a party in celebration to which all my friends were invited. Stan arrived, rolled round tightly by a long blue scarf, looking like the Michelin tyre man, and occasionally unwinding himself with great gusto. The critics came too, and were entertained to lunch in College but I kept clear of them. In those days it was not done to meet them. However it must have been a very good lunch, for Balliol gave me an extra £100 as well as my Life Membership of the S.C.R., and I felt extremely well treated.

Fifteen years later when Stan had been awarded the C.B.E. he wrote to me, 'Among my congratulations I had a nice letter from Julian Huxley . . . and just as I was beginning to feel very grand, explaining to myself that doubtless silence from this exalted source in the past was caused by a feeling of reticence and that now I could look for a few nobs among my associates I came to this, "All best wishes for 1950, and your work. I saw your murals in Holywell recently for the first time, and much liked them." At any rate times are improving . . . One no longer needs to have recourse to hairy skins . . . in order to come by what properly belongs to your brother. The Jacob of today need only be an artist, and have a brother who is a better one, at once to acquire the honours the other should have had.'

His irritation at our being confused is only too clear but he ended, 'Don't mention the *faux pas*, he meant well', and that is how I try to suffer it when on occasion I am introduced as the painter of my brother's pictures.

We had spent two years in Oxford attached to Balliol, enjoying the wonderful 'live and let live' atmosphere free from prejudice, and I could genuinely appreciate the purposes and justification of the university. Before we left I climbed to the top of the Bodleian, and saw Whitham Woods as a dark background to the spires and towers of Oxford, then still undisturbed, or spoilt by today's 'progress'. Neither had the 'wind of change' then penetrated to the high table of the college. I remember a comment of Kenneth Bell from which I gleaned that he seemed to feel some contempt for members of the university who felt the urge to move out into the world.

The time had come anyhow for us to move out. Having re-booked our rooms in Oxford for mid-September with Mrs. Hancock, we left, not in the usual way through the windows, but formally, by the door under the stable arch.

11

Burdens and Tree Cottage

1931–1936

SOON after we married Ursula had seen a copy of *Queen* at the hairdresser's, and copied out the address of an unfurnished farmhouse to let in Dorset. I too was greatly attracted by the sound of it, and feeling there was no time to lose she left next morning for Waterloo to catch the train to Semley, thence by bus to Shaftesbury and on to Compton Abbas; finally a little walk down Buddens lane towards Twyford, and there was Burdens Farm House. It had been empty for some time, and looked gaunt and starey-eyed. None the less we loved the place on sight, and took it from the farmer, Ivor Day for 10 shillings a week, plus rates. I even went so far as to draw up a gentleman's agreement (stamped) with Ivor, one of the clauses permitting us to hang our washing in the orchard. At first we got our drinking water carried up to us on a yoke from the forge, and our baths were heated by lighting up the copper in a large and draughty kitchen. This opened onto the farmyard with its cows, pigs, chickens, wild cats and a not inconsiderable number of rats. The garden sloped towards the shadow of Melbury beacon, and in the distance Shaftesbury perched on its rocky headland overlooking Blackmore Vale. It was in this place that we spent all our spare time for fourteen years, and to which we departed in the summer of 1936 to wait for the time when the arrival of our child would take us back to Oxford in the autumn.

Looking through the catalogue of my retrospective exhibition at Reading, I see that my picture 'Blackmore Vale' (City Art Gallery, Manchester) was painted in 1931. In fact at that time we were renting a cottage just outside Shaftesbury. On one of our evening walks we followed leafy French Mill Lane for some distance before turning back. Had we gone on round one more corner we would have come in sight of Twyford and Burdens, to which by the next summer we had moved. The next five years, before the birth of our daughter, confirmed our love of the place. There were many and varied moods which whatever form they took, came to rest at Burdens.

One stormy evening we strolled along a lane, and saw a board stuck in the hedge on which was painted 'To Rebbick's Farm'. We were halted by a gate at the end of the track and saw across to the farm where a man was looking around him, as farmers do towards darkness. In a nervous halting why I called over to him, 'You are well in the wilds out here'. 'And why not?' he replied in a quiet Dorset voice. Encouraged by this we opened the gate, and went across to him, and after some conversation he said—'Won't you come in, and sit down?'. Dorset hospitality on a Sunday evening has its own character. Before we realized what was happening Mr. Rebbeck invited us to draw up our chairs to a lovely supper prepared by the family. With the excitements and sounds of the farm life going on all round, one felt that the very cows were breathing down our necks.

Waking in the morning to the freshness of these little valleys with Melbury across the meadows, was likewise a heartening experience. Such another place was Inkpen in Berkshire with its beacon, the home of my brother-in-law John Bradshaw where my friend Bingo, a dalmatian, would cover miles to make up for our lack of them while we stopped to look at the views.

Feelings arising from these walks were not necessarily the occasions for a canvas, rather the seed ground. I might have spied out and pegged down in my mind something seen between gaps in a hedge, or from some almost inaccessible place, to return to it later, loaded with my materials. Backwards and forwards I would go to these places for as long as the sun would remain not excessively, but reasonably, in the same place. I knew by habit when he was giving me the slip, and I could no longer honourably continue chasing the events in a particular 'plain air' painting. Occasionally I have had to postpone a painting until the following year, or for four years as in the case of 'Sashes Meadow'. Not that I was a purist about the subtleties some feel regarding changing light, but I very rarely touched a landscape indoors. Nor was I just a summer landscape painter, as I painted many in the winter, near enough to home to slip in for a coffee. and warm-up. Like my brother, I have always taken great care in setting out my pictures on the canvas at the start, using a sharply pointed pencil which disappears behind the painting as I progress.

It was and is also a habit of mine not to jump to conclusions, rather to wait, and make little drawings for reference. If one or other of them returned to mind with increased insistence I was left with no doubt that I was wholly involved with that idea. When this happened it nearly always turned out to be as my brother would say 'a good one'. It was a way of testing my feelings and convictions.

I was confirmed in these again when I saw after many years some of my early pictures at my retrospective exhibition at Reading. One of these called 'The Drayman' was only 12 inches by 15½, and I remembered how it had come about. It was in the early twenties when Percy, Stan and I were just entering Turville on one of our walks from Cookham when I noticed a drayman perched high up on his seat, as was the habit in those days. I made no comment at the time, but clearly it made a strong impression on me. Quoting from the catalogue I read that my little picture was exhibited at Huddersfield Art Gallery (opening exhibition 1939), Cairo(!) (British Council International Art Exhibition 1947), Astley Chatham Art Gallery, Stalybridge (Annual Exhibition of Contemporary Art, 1953) and permanently at the Grove Art Gallery, Sheffield. This is a long way for a small brewer's drayman to have travelled. I feel it is a significant echo from the past.

Of course I add composition and pattern to these original drawings, but I like to keep as closely as possible to them, preferring my subjects not to be arranged, but of natural, or at least accidental events. The 'Sheep Pen' and 'Shutting up geese' arose from my regular employment helping at that time on the farm. Once I painted a little chest of drawers in my room with a loosely hinged mirror leaning over as though it was looking down into a half opened drawer below. This was illustrated in one of London's society weeklies with the caption 'An exercise in the sordid'. Yet I loved painting it, and hoped my landlady who took so much trouble over me, would not see it.

There are some crises in one's life that pass undetected, and this most assuredly could be said of my life after completing the Balliol murals. I gave no thought for the morrow, and this was probably my best protection against worry. If anxious about my work, my answer was to get out, and draw some trees, or have another go at Melbury. How many times I tried to master Melbury Beacon it would be difficult to say. Certainly it was my Mount St. Victoire. But I regarded it as a challenge, not a defeat, and certainly not a halt sign.

Nevertheless I was very pleased and not a little surprised just before leaving Burdens in September 1936 to receive a letter from Dudley Tooth setting out in detail a contract, providing a regular sale for my pictures, for me to sign when he returned from holiday. I reinforced this by sending him two large Dorset landscapes which sold almost by return of post. A little later at Oxford when my attention was wholly directed to Ursula, I received another letter from Dudley cancelling the project in which he wrote, 'I now see that he (my brother Stanley), does not think it a good plan that you should both show at the same gallery. I am afraid I shall have to cancel the idea'.

Although it was Stan who told me that Dudley had originally suggested the contract I never attempted to take my brother to task about this. It would have made no difference had I done so. That classic comment of Alice, our servant, to my mother—'I know my place, Mum' expressed my feelings. Later, when Tooth's was bombed, they held Stan's next show at the Leicester Galleries, to which I had now returned and Stan wrote to me rather apologetically to say that he had not been told about it. It had not worried me for I have never subscribed to the theory that any artist, be he brother or otherwise, can do harm in this way; only good can arise out of being in good company.

Tooth's letter created a crisis in my affairs that left its mark on me for life, but almost before I had had time to take it in, the telephone bell rang where I was staying with the Duncan Macgregors, and it was Dr. Raymond Greene to tell me that Gillian had been born at midday, October 21st 1936. Of course, I could not be anything else but happy on a day like that.

Earlier in the year we had answered an advertisement which took us to 'The Crown' at Lower Basildon for a weekend while we negotiated the purchase of Tree Cottage, Bethesda Street, at Upper Basildon. Our arrival there now was something of a triumphal progress, Louis Behrend having sent his Daimler to collect us. With Ursula to think of and Gillian in Nurse Cressey's arms, I kept the shadow of Tooth's letter in the back of my mind as far as I was able, and anyway for the next five weeks, not only the baby and Ursula but myself and all my troubles became subservient to Nurse Cressey. Happily I did not feel that there was anything unusual or out of place in Gillian being there, and have since formed the opinion that there is no break with the past when one becomes a father, but I admit that when Nurse Cressey came down in the evening in her snow-white uniform, I took a surreptitious glance under the tablecloth at my hands as we sat down to supper. Still she was splendid, and a perfect father's nurse as well. What went on upstairs was no business of mine, but downstairs I spent some little time assuring her that the abdication of Edward VIII was completely constitutional. She would not believe me.

Sometimes I crept along to take a peep at Gillian in her cot, only to be greeted by a wall of jet blackness, and not a sound of her. However at 2 a.m. Nurse Cressey brought her in and passed her over me to Ursula. Again I felt no surprise to wake to this experience. To the uninitiated, Gillian having her feed sounded as if she was going down for the third time in a flood of milk, to the accompaniment of gurgles of satisfaction, and delight, till overcome by sleep she was carried back to her cot all unawares, as Stan and I had been all those years before.

Apprehension has been a bugbear of mine all my life. I never doubted that all being well the mother is supreme in dealing with the child and that her subtle and mysterious intuition can never be replaced, but still I felt the father's role was to roam round the house at night, and keep the beasts of prey at bay. Happily I practised this mostly in nightmares, and only on one occasion in reality.

One night at Burdens I entered the scullery, a bricked-up affair, leading out of the kitchen, and was horrified to find myself confronted by a doe rat. With a babe in arms in the house, the implication of a doe rat in search of food was not lost on me. I was very frightened, and slammed the door against her escape into the house. Then I took up a position at one end of the scullery, while she watched me from her corner. She was at bay, but so was I! Soon she moved off behind a cupboard and I crept up to it. Looking over the top was like looking down a crevasse between the cupboard and the wall, but I could just see, coming up to the light and looking straight at me, her evil eyes. Fortunately there was a board handy. I held it end-on above the crack, and with the speed and strength borne of desperation, plunged it down on top of her. Silence followed. I breathed again, and the doe rat breathed her last.

The moment Gillian began to crawl I sawed off the end of our bed to make a gate for the top of the stairs. But on another occasion when my apprehensive nature demanded instant action, it was a nearby beekeeper who came to the rescue. A swarm of bees had settled on a cherry tree near my daughter's white pram in which she lay asleep, and I saw her in my mind's eye blanketed beneath them. But the bee-keeper deftly brushed them off the tree on to a board along which they faithfully followed one another into a skip.

Burdens always remained our spiritual home in spite of its roughness and readiness. We could not settle at Tree Cottage in the same way. Soon after our arrival there a carrier pigeon flew in at the kitchen door, and settled on the cupboard where he stayed for two or three days, so that I had someone to talk to when I came down in the mornings. Whether he was going through the same mental process as I, I cannot say, but finally, after carrying out his drill he flew off and disappeared to the west. I think, had it not been for Gillian, we too would have taken to the skies, circled round three times, and made a bee line for Burdens.

12

Upper Basildon
1936–1939

WE were now in midwinter at Upper Basildon. Three days a week I voyaged up to the Royal College of Art where I had continued as Professor of Painting throughout my time at Balliol. November fogs, and other night hazards made it difficult for me to find my way home, but I am a born countryman, and I loved the darkness, the light of the stars, and the occasional complainings of the owls. By day, looking through the tracery of the bare trees below us I noticed parts of the Chilterns and the Berkshire downs coming into view, and my spirits rose. High up above the Thames Valley on clear days one could see Inkpen Beacon and, by climbing a tree near Kiln farm, it was said one could see the Needles.

Several of our windows were newly leaded. With the exception of one in the old part of the cottage, which had G. Evans 1888 scratched on it, we had them changed, so that when opened we felt we were out of doors. In winter I painted and drew many pictures from these windows, but for my larger pictures I had a little Colt studio put up in the garden. When I entered it for the first time I hated it so much that I knocked it about, and messed it up to get it more in sympathy with my feelings for painting in odd corners, or bedrooms, indoors. The fact is I am no 'studio' artist and never have been, a hang-over from Cookham days. My brother also had a large studio built in his garden at Lyndworth, Cookham, but merely stored his drawings in it, and preferred to work indoors.

As the weather improved, on bicycle, or on foot, I found many places to my liking, and would batten down my easel by methods of my own. Nothing would move it nor me while I was painting, and what I painted was not only what I saw, but what I was feeling and hearing. Country sounds going on all round me put me in a happy mood, and got into my pictures. Blessed with good health I was ready to walk two or three miles a day to be satisfied with the feel of a place. Bare patches, where I wore away the grass with my 'runways' backwards and forwards would begin to appear, marking my open-air studios, and enabling me to find my place again next time without trouble. I was content to be on my own, but equally pleased if company found me out. Once a labourer, coming up from behind me, said very quietly 'I am liking that'. I enjoy and need encouragement, and am by no means self-sufficient like some painters. In fact I rather distrust their independence, being myself quite prepared to make modifications as the result of comments, provided they are not so severe as Stan's 'Hullaballoo about nothing'. But he listened sometimes himself; in particular he made a drastic change from his original large wash composition for the Burghclere altar-piece on the advice of Gwen Raverat, his old friend from Slade days.

I did not come to Tree Cottage unknown. For some years before I had been established as a typically English artist to which a number of reviews in the national press at that time testify. For instance, in a cutting from *The Times* I read, 'Mr. Spencer is the kind of artist who could only happen in England. In his most ambitious painting "The Cotswold Farm" . . . horses, carts, poultry, pigeons and hurdles are assembled in a remarkably interesting way . . . without which the picture would have lost the sharp flavour which makes it so English'. The same theme runs through all the reviews, Konnody in *The Observer* writing 'Mr. Gilbert Spencer is an artist of pure English lineage', and Bone, in the *Manchester Guardian* 'Very much an English painter'. *The Sunday Times* (Rutter) was perhaps less complimentary, but equally clear about my nationality: 'The good old English way of muddling through!' *The Spectator* summed it all up, 'Mr. Spencer's work is English of the English'.

Today with travel so widespread, a different kind of 'English of the English' might have emerged, but it seems to have become fearful or ashamed of its own natural vitality. Much as I have loved the French impressionists I have never felt it was my business to uproot my essentially native characteristics. This was understandable fifty or more years ago when the pattern of life at Cookham was almost as restricted for us as it must have been for the primitives, but I have never grown out of feeling that way.

Friends soon began to find their way to Tree Cottage and the first was James Ritchie, a friend of the Bradshaws, whom we called Jam Pot James because of his unique wedding present. A shy but attractive young man in a yellow waistcoat, he arrived with a large dripping cake, for the baby we presumed! Later we went to his wedding in Marlow, with the band of the Oxfordshire and Buckinghamshire Light Infantry playing under the trees. He was killed at Hazebrook barely two years later, guarding the Dunkirk beaches.

His visit was soon followed by one from Lawrence Binyon and his wife who to our surprise had walked over from Aldworth. We were much touched by this, and delighted by the many invitations we had afterwards to visit them in their lovely home at Westridge. There would be croquet on the lawn with their daughters Helen and Peg, while their grandchildren ran around the beautiful garden situated on the very edge of the ridge as it spilled down to Goring Gap far below with a felt but unseen beauty. I was tempted to ask Binyon to let me draw him, and wish now I had asked him as he had a very fine head and was an understanding man. But I was over-anxious in case it should prove one of those drawings I could not turn round to show.

When Stan came over to see us on his own we were glad to be able to mix him in with some of the friends we had made in the village so that family arguments were avoided. He did not like disagreements, but I was not prepared to allow all his assertions, and it was much happier to be able to introduce him to Leslie Hayward, the illustrator, and the Miss Jones who were deeply interested in his selections from the Bible, and the use he made of Cookham. We were able to look into Ursula's concordance to check the story of Zacharias and Elizabeth which picture he began before he was twenty, but there was no concordance at home for us then. My father took its place.

Other friends of those days to meet Stan were the Scott James family. Ann and Mary both wrote reviews for the national press and I felt there was something of the same relation between them as between Stan and me except that Mary was better able than I to turn aside and accept calmly and good humouredly the subtle distinctions between her and her sister. She called one morning to find me in a white heat of rage because a chairman introducing me to an audience had credited me with several of my brother's masterpieces. One resents these mistakes, but they can and do happen. I was a hard working painter who loved the job but I always realized there would be difficulties following the same trade as Stan, and that I could not survive returning to Cookham as he wished. Later he liked to claim that my marriage had 'ruined' me, but this went in one ear and out of the other. Indeed I have never understood why, because I had bought a cottage and an acre of ground through the Halifax Building Society, reinforced by a banker's reference, and kept a bicycle instead of a car in the garage, that it should have been thought by some extremists of my profession that I had become conventional, or 'married money'. It is true that Lady Ottoline had to be handled a little delicately when I told her about Ursula after my seemingly unorthodox way of life—eighteen odd domiciles since leaving Cookham—and that she was surprised at the gusto with which I decided to marry. 'Anyway, dear Gil', she said, 'you have married a lady'. Indeed I had. Ursula was resolute and strong, with perfect reactions to meet all occasions, except money! 'Gather ye rosebuds while ye may', 'Say not the struggle nought availeth', were her way, and she lived it up to the hilt all her life.

Thus it was perhaps that she did not recognize the nature of the business of two bowler hatted men who followed her into Tree Cottage one afternoon as she was pushing Gillian home. I returned from the Royal College of Art to find little notes pinned to the soft furnishings, reminding me of Holywell days, and Duncan Macgregor's happier messages pinned to the furniture. These as I explained to Ursula were of a different kind.

Next morning I went to Reading to see the collector of taxes. He briefly explained to me the seriousness of my position adding, 'I don't want to send you to prison'. It proved easier than I had expected to soften him, because in quite a different tone of voice he next said, 'You are Gilbert Spencer, aren't you?' Apparently he knew and liked my work very much, and also my brother's. The conversation flowed happily away from finance, and I discovered that he painted himself and tried every year to go to France and visit the Louvre. But when I believed that all was well for me, he pulled me back to earth as I got up to leave. 'You will be all right while I am here', he said, 'but God help you when Moon comes!' Somehow we must have circumvented 'Moon' too but it was pleasant when I was later elected as hon. member of the Reading Guild of Artists to find my friend, the tax collector, already a member.

I was even more pleased when I was invited to become a vice-president of the Basildon Cricket Club, although it was not as a cricketer that I had been asked. None the less I immediately fancied myself addressing a wrapped audience at some cricket function, extolling the virtues of a game which has given a new word expressive of fair play to the English language, or making a well judged comparison of village cricket long ago to village cricket today. With this lofty prospect in view I wandered down the lane to the Basildon recreation ground ready to mix the pleasures of watching cricket, and lying in the shade of elms. The Reading West Indians were batting on a 'deal board' wicket, their stroke play well nigh perfect, and the only convincing proof I had that they were not the West Indian Eleven proper playing at Basildon, was that I knew the latter were at that moment playing at Lords. After two hours of this sort of play I began to find it monotonous, and apparently the village did too, because no one was left to watch except Mr. and Mrs. Griffiths and myself.

GILBERT SPENCER, R.A.

Cricket on Cookham Moor when I was a boy was different, hazardous in fact. During the week the pitch shared its existence with cows and geese, and their attentions reduced it to a bowler's paradise. Few visiting batsmen stayed at the wicket a moment longer than they could help! By way of 'dressing rooms' there were only the ditches round the fringe of the moor, covered with chickweed. Into these a batsman might occasionally hit the ball with great advantage to his score if he kept running, until one or other of the fieldsmen had the presence of mind to call 'lost ball', after which Fred Ducket would patiently carry on the search with his rake.

Injuries were surprisingly few having regard to the dangers. A powerful sweep to the leg took the ball on its flight to the boundary, straight across the main road to the village. On one occasion a gentleman cycling by had his boater sliced off as clean as a whistle without touching a hair of his head. Perhaps because of such incidents, or because we produced a fast bowler off whom, on Cookham Moor, Bradman himself would have found it difficult to score, Colonel Ricardo decided the time had come to play elsewhere. Accordingly he gave the village a lovely cricket field at his home, Lullabrook Manor, with every kind of accessory. No more were we to face the demon bowling of 'Rasher' Hatch without gloves or pads, although at first we were inclined to think such protection rather soft. Weekend house parties at the manor included a fair sprinkling of good cricketers, but there is no class distinction in cricket, and deserving Cookham talent always found a place in the teams. I was picked once for the Second XI against Maidenhead Post Office, and scored thirteen!

Those were the days when the best form of local government was benign squiredom. In our case the conservatism of Colonel Ricardo was an excellent foil to the austere Liberalism of Sir George Young. It was Colonel Ricardo who intervened when he heard that the chapel was to be sold to a fishmonger, and gave it to the village for the free library rather than that it should acquire a 'fishy reputation'. My father was delighted with that little touch. Today its reputation is not in doubt. Visitors come from all over the world to see a permanent exhibition of my brother's pictures which, thanks to the 'Friends of Stanley Spencer' now hang there.

It would have been pleasant to be able to skip in time from my memories of peacetime cricket at Cookham before the First World War, to watching cricket at Basildon after the Second World War, but doubts as to Munich were now filling us with foreboding, and on our return to Burdens for my summer's painting in 1939 we were prepared for the worst. On September 3rd we walked across the fields to Compton Church, and there heard Mr. Chamberlain's moving broadcast that we were at war with Germany again. Although a socialist, I greatly admired Neville Chamberlain, and my reactions on hearing him then were that 'he nothing common did nor mean, upon that memorable scene'. When a member later called across the floor of the House of Commons 'Speak for England' my sympathies were with Mr. Chamberlain who had striven to his utmost to save us from what he feared was coming. Munich became his personal cross.

13

From Basildon to Grasmere

1939–1945

AS a young man in 1913 I had seen the whole British Army—all three-hundred-and-sixty-five-thousand of them—dusty and tired, with General French on horseback at their head, march through Cookham on manœuvres. My father had prophesied that the distant bombardment coming from Cockmarsh hill would bring thunder, while the excitable Charlie Warren declared the army would be passing through the village all day. Bands were playing 'Tipperary', the sound of it rising and falling, as they passed out of earshot across the moor. A year later 'Tipperary' was to encourage those same men as they embarked for France to meet the greatest military machine ever known to man at that time. Yet ignorant of the meaning of modern war, I remember calling down jocularly to friends on the river below Cookham Bridge 'Namurs no more!', and laughing at this feeble piece of drollery. Then there had been the feeling that it would be all over by Christmas. Now, in 1939 it was felt that the war was never going to start at all.

The strange stillness of those first months resulted in an extension of my vacation from the Royal College, so that I was able to continue painting peacefully at Burdens, until the difficulty of blacking it out—it was too full of character and cracks for anything of that kind—and the danger of being regarded as a questionable sort of 'quisling' decided us to return to Basildon. In 1914 misgivings between people of that kind never crossed our minds, but now, even in far-off Dorset, pitchfork in hand, on top of a rick, one sensed the defeatist at work among the helpers.

At Basildon I joined the Local Defence Volunteers—splendidly redubbed the 'Home Guard' by Churchill—and soon found myself patrolling the village, reviving memories of my smartness and efficiency in the first war, cleaning and polishing my rifle, the old 'ipe' as it was called, with Jimmy Cowell, of the Duke of Cornwall's Light Infantry sticking his thumb in the breach while I peered down the barrel at the lovely glistening bore, as it coiled away from me.

In this stalemate period of the 'Phoney War' it was decided to re-open the Royal College of Art, and I took to box-ing and cox-ing between Twyford and Bedford Square where my brother Percy lived. They were still digging trenches in the Square garden when we heard our first sirens. I remember people running light-heartedly for cover in the lulled state of mind created by the unreal atmosphere of those first months. The blackout added to this dream-like quality bringing with it what was the loveliest of experiences on our walks through the city at night, that of seeing St. Paul's and the Thames illumined by a full moon instead of blanketed by the starless red glare we knew in our far off Brixton days.

Shortly before Dunkirk, Churchill's roar as he called it, woke us to our danger, and sharpened our morale at a critical time. The college closed, and we returned each to his allotted post for the defence of Britain—myself to the guard room next door to the 'Beehive' Inn at Basildon.

Earlier I had seen queues of children at Paddington, each labelled for safety, holding hands, and clutching their few precious belongings; and arriving home one evening, had found Ursula throwing herself into two new-found responsibilities, Colin and his sister Jean. Later, when on guard between the 'Beehive' and the guard room I was asked by a soldier carrying a suitcase, and accompanied by his mother where he should take her, I called over, 'Try Tree Cottage'. When I got home I found not surprisingly 'Old Mrs. Nutley-come-in-at-the-door', as we called her, had already had supper, and gone to bed.

We liked Mrs. Nutley. She helped about the house, helped over a glass of stout with a bit of sewing, and brought with her those motherly touches which come with experience. She came to us out of the docks which by then were an inferno, but though we laid in a supply of stout so that she should not be tempted to return to them, it was to no avail. She missed her visits to the 'local' and could not stand the quiet and darkness of Upper Basildon.

The news that over a hundred German planes had been shot down, was brought to us by Louie Trinder our maid, when she roused us one morning, but we did not at first grasp the full significance. We had had a slightly disturbed night, sirens sounding fitfully, and one or two near 'unpleasantnesses', and were pleased to go to sleep again. Later we heard Mr. Churchill's dramatic tribute to the 'Few' which must vie for fame with Nelson's 'England expects'. As a sleeping partner in more meanings than one to the Battle of Britain, I could but return to the 'Beehive'.

The sickening futility of war for those on its fringes only emerges clearly in retrospect. In those next months I was both to see the pall of black smoke which ringed round Coventry through which the German bombers searched their way, and to hear wave after wave of our own bombers as they passed over Tree Cottage on their way to find their targets in Germany.

We were to experience another contradiction when the Royal College of Art re-opened its doors at the Queen's Hotel at Ambleside. There, nearby Liverpool was in flames, but we were to know Grasmere as Wordsworth had known it, and to hear that strange note ringing round the frozen lake as its waters lowered —rather than the wail of sirens.

Spurred on by a talk at the college by an air raid precautions officer from Liverpool I duly reported to the Home Guard at Ambleside. It was unavoidable that a large section of the population could not be used in the war, but it was a brilliant stratagem on the part of the government to make us behave so ridiculously, and yet succeed in making us immensely proud of what we were doing! No words can describe my own pride at being able to crawl a hundred yards without my behind showing above the sky line. I stormed the heights of Nabscar, helped to restore the defences of Windermere when knocked down by the sheep, relived my moonlight walks in London patrolling the fells above the glistening lakes below, and by a mistaken choice of parades I found myself shying live hand grenades at the side of Loughrigg.

After such daring exploits as these I would return to Ursula and Gillian safely in bed at Ladywood, the home of Professor de Selincourt. Ursula had been a pupil of his at Birmingham, and he had invited us to go to live with him. My companions in the Home Guard seemed to think I would find him a difficult man. So he was at times, but I deeply respected him. He is the only man not only to have told me that I was being perfectly ridiculous, but to convince me that I was!

The organization of our days at Ladywood worked well. The sound of Dr. de Selincourt's firm footsteps across the hall after breakfast back to his study and his books on Wordsworth was the signal to send me upstairs to my room where I was painting a version of the Tolpuddle Martyrs. I had fatigue duties too, including scrubbing the kitchen floor. I worked flat out, and finished it flat out too, feeling exactly like the orderly spread-eagled on the floor in one of Stan's Burghclere murals. Equally active, Arnold Goldsborough, who, with his family, had also found a haven at Ladywood, was careering all over the country keeping musical engagements while his wife and Ursula busied themselves organizing the running of the house.

There were so many children and grandchildren around—Heather, Christopher, Mary, Ann, Robin, Maria, and Gillian—that we were provided with a wonderfully effective armour with which to protect ourselves from the grimness of war, where it seemed often that we were heaving at a relentless vacuum. Liverpool was still smouldering when the byways and lanes around Grasmere began to fill up with heavily loaded and camouflaged lorries, which stayed stuck, apparently abandoned, until by D-day, which was still three years away, they stretched nose to tail all the way down to the beaches. Meanwhile with the children to anchor us, we learnt from them how to accept our lot and to occupy ourselves with peace-time ploys. Slowly I disclipined myself to take an interest in the life, and lovely surroundings at Ladywood. I never came to terms with the mountains, and treated them as sky, but in this way I managed to paint 'Redbank' from the balcony, and other landscapes from, and around, the

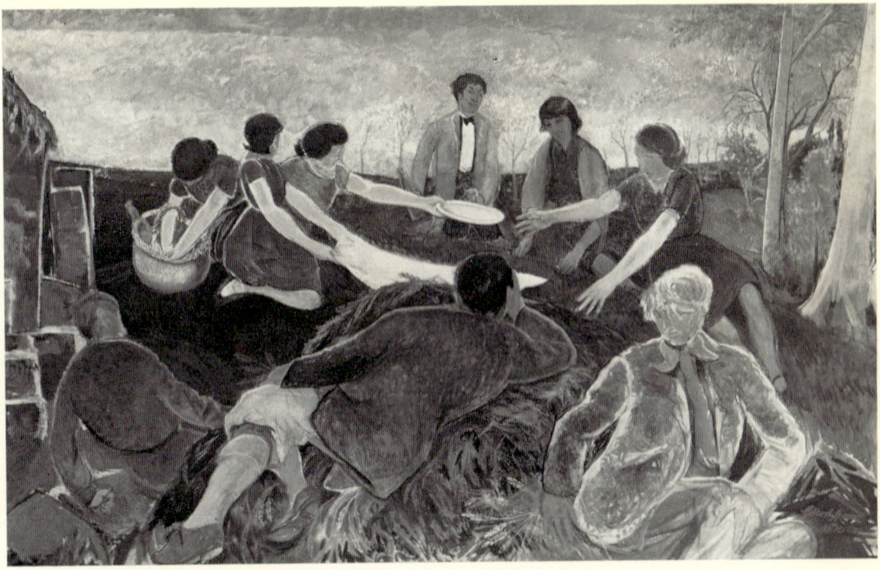

5a The Rick Party (1971)

5b 'Burdens' with Melbury Beacon (1943)

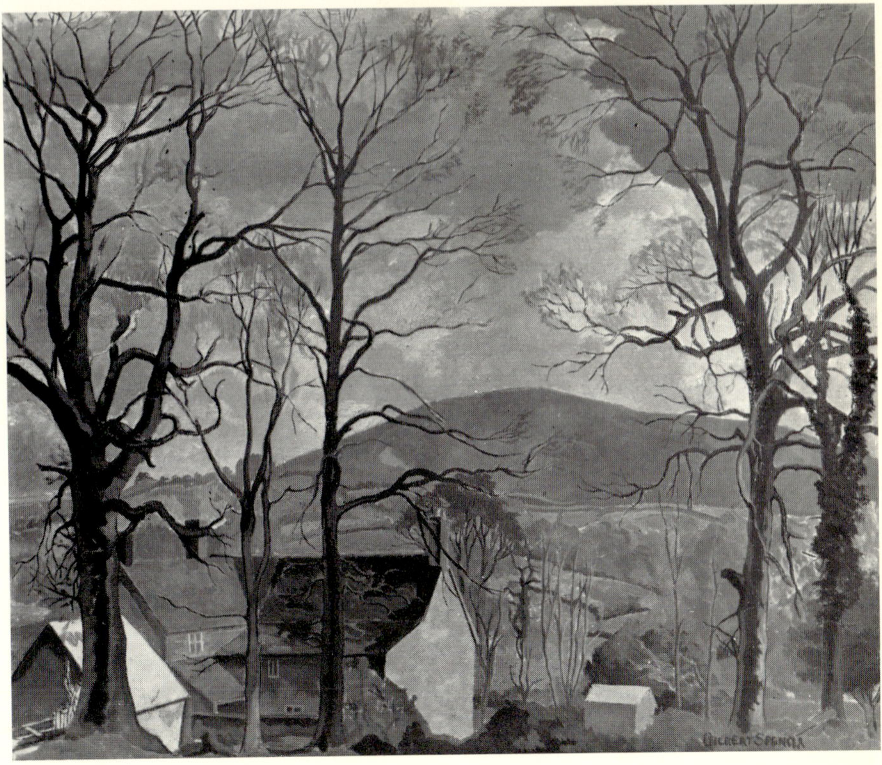

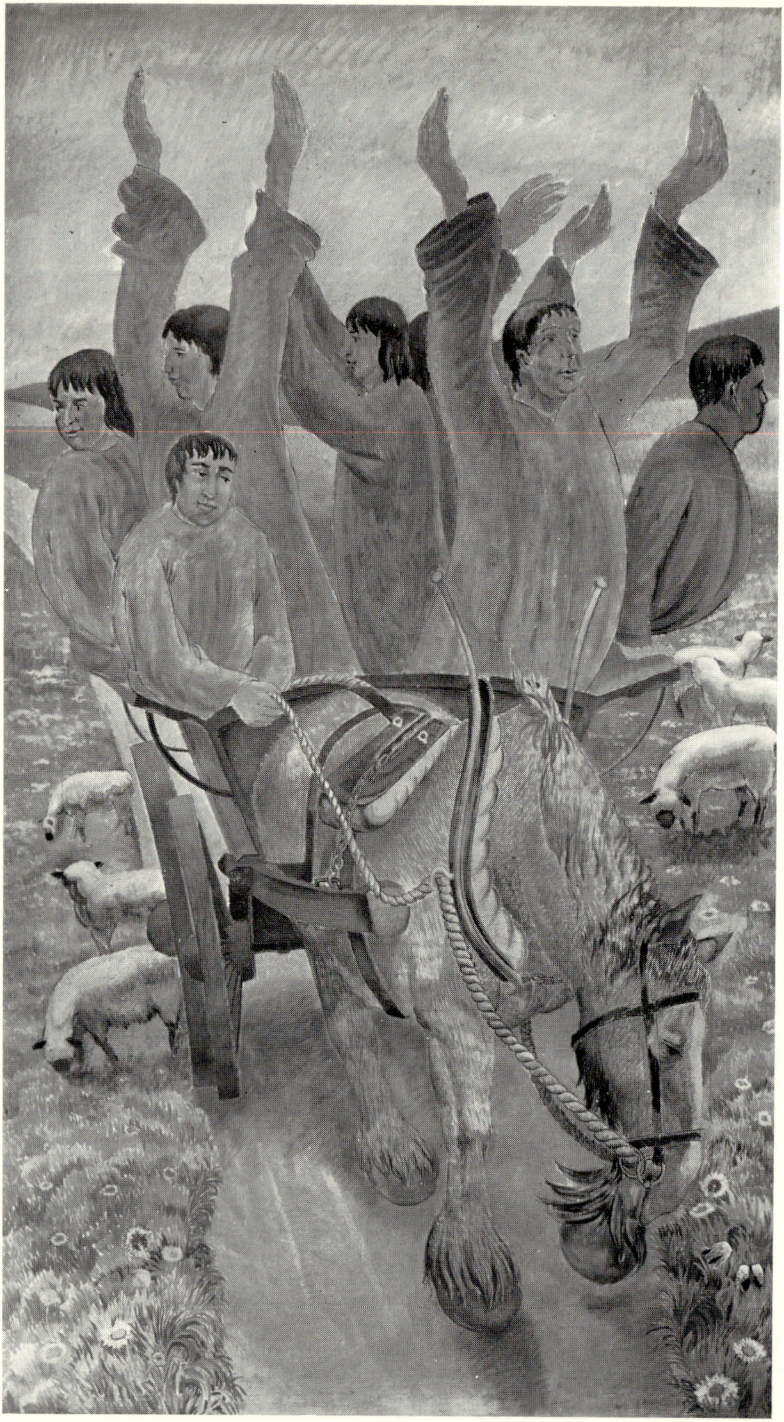

6 Detail from the Balliol Murals (1936):
Monks in the Farm Wagon

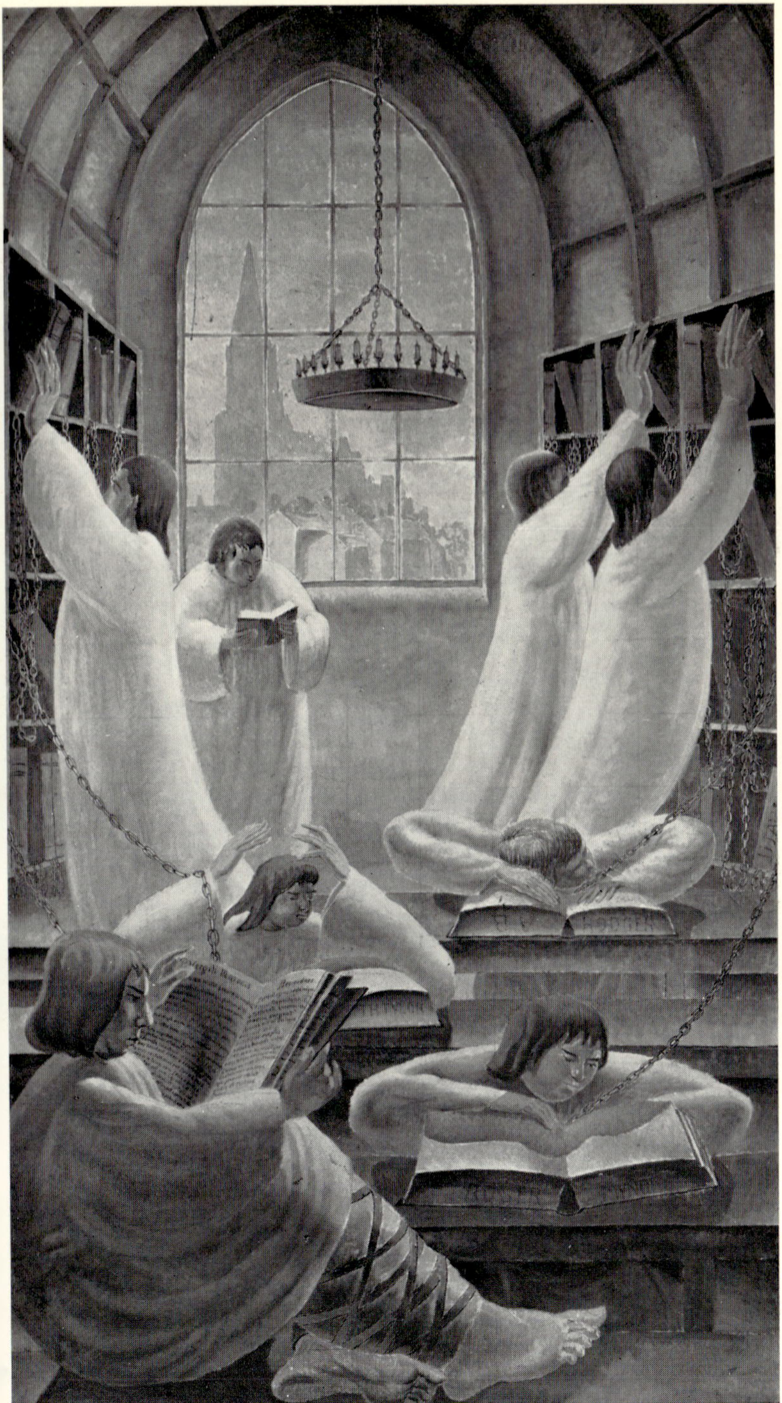

7 Detail from the Balliol Murals (1936):
The Library

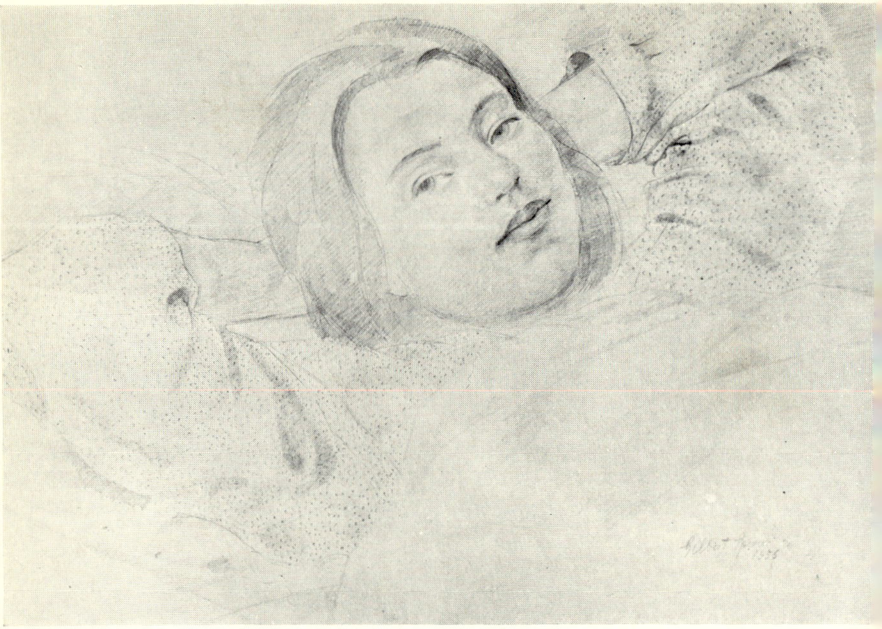

8a Gillian 'A Day in Bed' (1951)

8b Suffolk Wagon (1958)

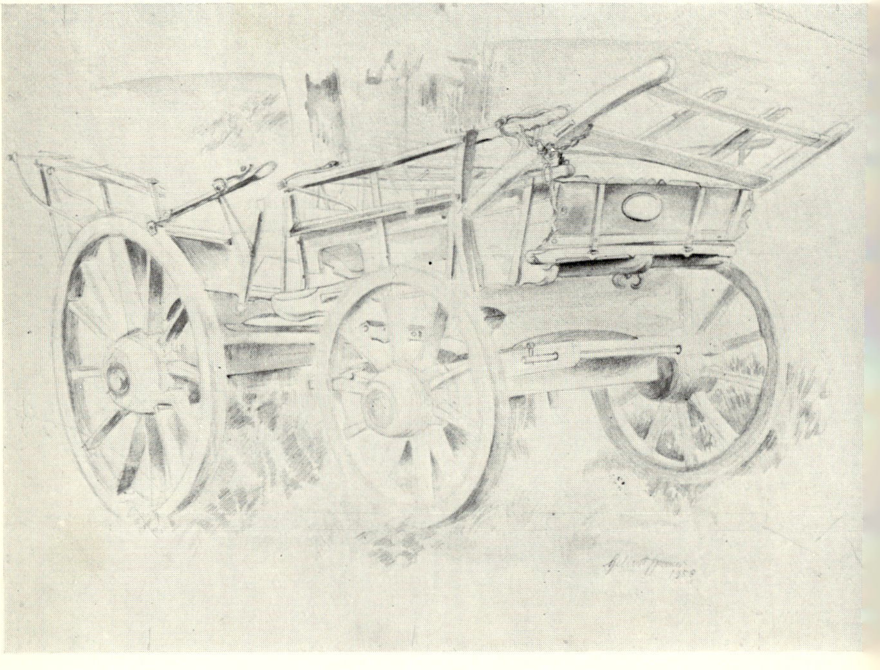

garden. I have none of these pictures left now. In 1943 I had a most successful show at the Leicester Galleries which brought a congratulatory telegram from Dr. de Selincourt when Ursula told him that I had sold everything.

While at Ladywood I crossed swords with a fellow professor whose religion I disliked as much as he did mine. The dislike hardened into a dispute about the interpretation of the terms of a scholarship. I raged about the house! Dr. de Selincourt told Ursula it was a form of madness, while his son, Oliver, said I was a long winded beggar, and Malcolm escaped from the house to climb Nabscar. When the whole family had become involved Dr. de Selincourt decided it was time to take a firm hand. I had drafted a report to the Board of Education, and he told me to bring it to his study. As I came away I could see through the window by his expression that he was not reading Wordsworth! Later I was pleased to hear that he agreed with my points, but thought it far too long and had reduced it to two sides of an ordinary sheet of paper. In the end the Principal rang me up, and made it plain I need take no further action. Nor did my colleague press his claim, but one or two friends at court warned me that the ministry had got the tabs on me for future reference. Stan wrote me some good elder brotherly advice, 'If I were you I would try to ignore what you find unpleasant in the folk around you, and *read* Wordsworth'.

I was never heavily employed by the War Artists Advisory Committee though my first war picture 'F4 Ward 36 Stationary Hospital' was joined in the War Museum by 'Grasmere Home Guard' and 'Troops in the Countryside'. I heard from Stan that, 'Jas Wood wrote me a letter all about your cows and soldiers painting, illustrated with careful drawings of different parts of it. I, as you know, always have my little prayer mat in my hand ready to prostrate myself before everything I have seen of yours, but I thought this war one was a very good one. I liked the assertion of peace in it; the soldiers being as peaceful as the cows. It was like what a rabbit might have seen and felt, looking from a field opposite, and that would not know the khaki suits, etc. had any other significance than the markings of the cows.'

In addition to these war pictures I was employed to do a number of portrait drawings. I liked to talk to my sitters to find out about them, and their decorations, but one of them was so old I could not get a line on him until he said he had been over fifty years with the same firm without absence for sickness, or for any other reason. When I told this to the barmaid at the hotel where I was staying, she raised her arms exclaiming, 'Lor, what a lack of imagination!'

Another of my sitters was a young man at the Birmingham Small Arms factory. He was very quiet, which I attributed to nervousness, so I asked the foreman about him. I had already seen a huge naval gun lying on its belly in a deep pit, and a forest of rifle barrels, like saplings, being watered with oil as they spun round to be bored. Apparently my young man had had his feet shackled, and allowed himself with acetylene welder in one hand, to be lowered, head first, at the end of a hawser, to rescue a mate trapped on the fringe of an inferno in a deep gun pit.

Returning from one of these war jobs to Ladywood I felt the need to broaden my technique. I decided that the freedom of the comic drawing would be a good outlet, and to use my Home Guard experiences for subject matter. In the end I produced twelve imperial sized cartoons, standing up most of the time to do them in order to gain greater freedom, and drawing from the shoulder. I used every imaginable trick; ink, pencil, water-colour, smudging with thumb and finger, and sometimes letting the colour run down voluntarily, trapping it just in time with a free line of which David Jones was such a master. I felt I knew the rules sufficiently well to break them, and I would defend those drawings up to the hilt. They were 'all out of me own 'ed', as Stan would say cockily of something of his he liked. They were first exhibited in Dr. de Selincourt's drawing-room where they did a useful social service entertaining his distinguished visitors. The rich content of his bookshelves appeared not to be unduly disturbed by the imposition of the cartoons, nor Dr. de Selincourt to be worried that the 'Prelude' should be obscured by 'You should have answered Friend, Fred!'or *Paradise Lost* lost behind 'I wish I was not home-guarding tonight.'

In due course I sent them to a publisher, on Joyce Carey's advice, but they were returned to me torn to ribbons, and it cost me a lot to have them repaired. This frightened me. I suppose they gave offence at the time, for as Gilbert Murray once said to Ursula, people behave very strangely in wartime. Today 'Dad's Army', which my cartoons preceded in character, is a household favourite but had it appeared in wartime it might not have been thought so funny. However, I recovered from my shock, and the cartoons were finally shown in London at the Artists International Association, David Low himself showing his appreciation by opening the exhibition.

The death of Dr. de Selincourt in 1943 was a great personal loss to us. I had painted his portrait, but I should have stretched it on a larger canvas to do him justice. Naturally it was his humanity which reached me more than his scholarship, and thus a last memory of him must be allotted to Gillian as she sat on his knee at breakfast.

Gillian: 'Pretend I am Mrs. Poofkins, and you don't know who I am.'

Dr. de Selincourt (very solemnly): 'How can I pretend you are Mrs. Poofkins if I don't know who you are?'

The rest of the war we spent between Ladywood and the Bield at Little Langdale, the home of our close friends Delmar Banner, the artist, and his sculptress wife, Josephine de Vasconsollas. It was there we experienced the relief of the Armistice. We climbed to the top of Whetherlam and saw the world at our feet whichever way we turned. With Gillian to share our joy, our sense of peace was complete when on reaching home she asked for her skipping rope.

14

Transition

1946–1949

LOOKING back now on those war years I think it was right for Jowett not to seek an alternative post and to re-open the R.C.A. at Ambleside, but for myself I might have been happier taking up some other job. Being wholly involved in the First World War had not undermined my ultimate aim to be an artist. With an established reputation I could safely have taken on some other war-work without fear of lowering my sights. But they were going to be lowered for me now.

On returning to London something of the same phoney atmosphere which one sensed at the beginning of the war seemed to grip the college again. This was finally explained in 1948 when Jowett announced his retirement as principal, telling me that Robin Darwin's appointment in his place was, he thought, a good one.

That the new principal was to be a man of action first showed itself in the staff being each issued with a Yale key for the lavatory. Hitherto there had been only one key available to us, and this always hung in the porter's lodge. The head janitor, Pascoe, who mixed a permanent smile with a dry humour to ease any embarrassment had attached the key to a block of wood, painting its face with gloss white, and adding in large black letters 'King George V'. Perhaps our Yale keys were an indication of the expected effect on our digestive organs of the changes at the College.

Soon a number of trestle tables arranged along the corridor outside my room were knee deep with administrative edicts, which I felt formed no part of my artistic responsibilities. But in this I was mistaken, and it was through this forest of legislation that I threaded my way to Darwin's room on receiving his summons. My reception was cool, amounting to studied indifference and he was highly discouraging about my staff, adding that he only knew Rodney Burn. I knew that they had been together in the camouflage establishment at Leamington during the war. Now, with his shirt sleeves rolled up Darwin conveyed to me at that unhappy meeting that he was in fighting mood, and with his parting shot he asked me to let him have a lay-out of my Department.

Disconsolately I wended my way back to my room and took another look at the flood of instructions on the trestle tables as I passed. They had risen considerably since I first saw them, and I felt twice confounded. However I got hold of as many sheets of cartridge paper as there were rooms in my Department, and having described large circles on each, spider web fashion, proceeded from the outer perimeter to the principal's room in the centre, to give him a picture of a full week's work covering my Department—the number of each room, the numbers of students in each room, the names of the staff on duty, numbers of models engaged, and finally I divided each day into three sections 9.30 a.m.-12.30 p.m., 2 p.m.-4 p.m., and 5 p.m.-6 p.m. I thought it was brilliant, and handed it to Pascoe to give to the Principal.

Next morning he happened to join me in the lavatory, but did not appear to see me. I felt a little uneasy, and thought, as from one porcelain to another, he might have passed the time of day with me.

Six months before I had been delighted to tell Ursula that I had been given a rise in salary from £300 to £500 after eighteen years. That this was only a necessary procedure on the part of the Ministry and the College enabling them to raise the salary of a future Head of Department three-fold was wholly unsuspected by me. In fact they already had their knives out for me. Now I was asked to present myself before the Governors who had never so much as seen me before. They had arranged themselves carefully. Mr. Wedgwood, a cousin of Darwin's, who had succeeded Lord Hambleden, was in the Chair, but he said nothing and made no impression on me. Away to the west sat Darwin casting his shadow like the setting sun, over my future. It was left to Sir Charles Tennyson from the wings in a kind of echo voice to tell me that I had been retired. That was all. In less than five minutes I had left the room.

There was a sequel to this when I received a letter from Robin Darwin, ten years later, after he had caught sight of me at my brother's funeral, almost embarrassing in the expressions of regret at the way I had been treated and adding, 'I am determined that your services to the College shall not be forgotten'. In fact they conveniently were! Instead my brother Stanley was appointed one of its first Fellows. That Stan accepted the honour in the circumstances did not altogether surprise me, but I think he did not fail to read my feelings when I told him to mind the train of his gown and 'not trip up in it'.

I had been tripped up myself good and proper. Returning to Tree Cottage to tell Ursula what had happened to me was dreadful. I knew that her constant and spirited outbursts 'Say not the struggle' etc. would not be on her lips this time. We sat in the kitchen bitterly aware that the gap between 'One picture sold, two more pictures painted' could not be bridged without the supplement to my income from the College. Upstairs on the landing sat Gillian's trunk roped and ready to be put on the train for Badminton School. Had I then told Ursula to untie the rope I felt she might have hung me with it!

I am not the kind of artist whose convictions regarding his inalienable right to self expression takes precedence over his family responsibilities, but where was I to turn? There are many sayings about doors opening, light after darkness, silver linings etc.; but that help should have come from the other side of the Border, still seems to me a most extraordinary twist of fortune.

Not so long before I had acted as assessor to the Scottish Education Authority in an examination for art students. It was an anxious task involving Edinburgh, Glasgow, Dundee and Aberdeen. I believe I struck an all-time record in 'fails', and Aberdeen had come off the worst of the lot. Accordingly when the Chairman of the Aberdeen School of Art commented at lunch that it was customary for the assessor to announce the results to the doughty Scots, dirks in stocking, and bagpipes at the ready, I nervously explained, hugging my marks to my chest, that I would first have to send my report to the Scottish Education Authority, and caught the night express back home.

There was in fact a complaint from Aberdeen that I had failed one student by only two marks. Heavens above! I might have ruined a promising young artist by this absurd method of giving marks for Fine Art, but I could not change them now myself. However I suggested that there must surely be machinery by which, with my approval, the result could be varied, and in due course I received a friendly letter thanking me for the care I had taken, and enclosing my fee.

I must have given a better impression than I thought because now another letter arrived from the Director of the Glasgow School of Art, Douglas Bliss, offering me the Headship of the Painting School, on condition the Governors gave their approval. I knew the importance of this last, after my experience at the R.C.A., and in fact Sir Charles Tennyson's 'echo voice' did carry up to Glasgow, and was heard expressing surprise that I should be offered the job. This was against all the rules—first to so-call 'retire' a man, and then try to impede his chances of further employment. In addition, I was up against intense feeling at the time among Scottish Nationalists that any key position should be offered to a Sassenach. I heard later that Hugh McDermid was ready to run his assassin's pen through me, should he ever meet me.

All in all, it was best that my reply should be sufficiently cautious and indifferent to conceal my hopes that I might get the job. But Bliss was a painter himself and knew my work, which he had reviewed in the *Scotsman*, and in due course I heard to my relief that his carefully worded recommendation had succeeded with the Governors. Soon my new suitcase, optimistically called a 'Revelation', had joined Gillian's school trunk on the landing in readiness for my own journey, and in next to no time I was waving farewell to Ursula on Pangbourne Station in the mood of Ford Madox Brown's famous picture.

I spent the night in a carriage with a Glasgow Irishman stretched full length on the seat opposite in his shirt sleeves, and with his shoes off. At Carlisle, which we reached at 3 a.m., I listened to an owlish voice drawling out the names of the stations that lay ahead. As the train pulled out the name 'Motherwell' was swallowed down with a great gulp of hot tea for which at that time, cold and miserable as I was, I would have given my eyes. I remember looking out of the carriage window just after and seeing a narrow strip of water in the chilly dawn and wishing I could run round and jump over it, to warm myself up. Afterwards I learnt that, could I have done so, I would have leapt over the Clyde.

After the open lowlands, came the gloom of Motherwell, and the tortuous approach to the tunnel of blackness which was Glasgow Central. Breaking clear from this dungeon I was dazzled and almost blinded by the pale and brilliant sunlight of Glasgow before her busy housewives got their fires going and put it out. But the light that had greeted me was an omen of the happy times to come.

15

Glasgow

1950–1952

HOPPING into a taxi which took me to 5 Princes Gardens, I was soon being welcomed by Douglas Bliss, the Director of the Glasgow Art School. His wife had gone south to see the children back to school so that we were both in the nature of Grass Widowers. However breakfast was cooked for me by his mother, in a wonderfully spacious kitchen, with wide windows from which I got my first view of Glasgow, its hills covered by houses hugging and hanging on to one another for dear life, interrupted by occasional classical style 'Greek Thompson' churches, and rising above all what I took at first to be the typically Scottish silhouette of the university. Later I was told, with the courtesy with which in time one became so familiar, that it was copied from Bruges.

After a few exchanges Bliss, looking at his gold half-hunter, left me to go to the school, telling me to follow him later. When my turn came to go, Mrs. Bliss, whom I sensed at once to be a wise and discerning lady, told me to 'Be yourself!' This was good advice and to shake off the effects of the night journey which had left me with a fellow feeling for the Glasgow Irishman, I went first to Gunn's, the famous Glasgow tailors, and got myself measured up for a new suit. James Gunn's brother himself took my measurements, and as he did so gave me interesting sidelights about 'Jimmy's' pictures, and sitters, and told me of his own deep interest in music. This made me feel much more myself and I was ready to face the Art School.

My experience has led me to believe that art students are universal levellers, and sure enough within a couple of hours I had settled down to some teaching as naturally as though I had just come out of Room A at the Royal College, and gone into Room B at the Glasgow School of Art, without noticing.

After a brief meeting with the Deputy Director, Jefferson Barnes, I went along the passage to meet Mr. Masson, the Secretary. I told him, in reply to his inquiry, that I had been at the R.C.A. for eighteen years, but that as far as I knew we did not have any papers there, and my only recollection of anything of the kind was being handed, half an hour or so after my arrival, an all too familiar buff coloured envelope from the Inland Revenue, by the Head Janitor. When I gave Mr. Masson the date and year of my birth, he seemed not merely surprised, but alarmed, and he was out of his door like a long dog, returning shortly with a form which he filled up for me there and then, and which I signed just in the nick of time to qualify for a pension. I still think gratefully of that occasion on my weekly visits to the Post Office.

At lunch across the road, I had the pleasure of meeting my staff. All seemed to me in good order, and there was no occasion for notices on trestle tables in the corridor outside my room known as the 'Hen Run', unless perhaps there might have been a direction to visitors coming to see me after dark, to cough loudly before switching on a light as they climbed the stairs in order to give fair warning to the lovers. Anything approaching what Darwin called my 'Solar System' would have been unnecessary here, and most unpopular with the students, though they were quite happy when I made some suggestions, as much for my own guidance as theirs, as to the groups in which they should work. William Armour, my deputy, and right-hand man, mentioned that there was no need for an 'E' at the end of the word 'group'! That would have wrecked me at the R.C.A. but here, students and masters alike, we were all in the same boat, and it was up to me to hold on to the tiller, watching for the occasional surprise or excitement, and keeping a sharp look out of course for shocks.

Unfortunately soon after my arrival, the boat did rock a little when I advised a young lady that I did not think that she would make much of a success in the painting school. She spun round, and shook her little fist at me, and in her rage threatened 'litigation'. I went down to find Bliss, and tell him what had happened, and asked whether I should write a letter to the girl's parents, as she seemed so young. He shuddered at the thought, and his eyebrows which were very mobile, shot up to their highest point as he replied; 'No, no. Don't do that! The Scots are very litigious. We will look into it', adding as was usual in time of trouble 'Go and see Barnes'.

About this time I learnt that Mr. Gowans, the Librarian, was distressed that *Picture Post* should have published a large photograph of a 'Cotswold Farm' over a bewilderingly unfair criticism on me by Munnings. When the identity of Mr. Gowans dawned on me any pain I felt about the attack was overcome by the pleasure of realizing that this was the Mr. Gowans whose little illustrated books on the Early Masters had set Stan on his tracks, and I was delighted to be taken along by Bliss to see him. He was getting old now, and not very efficient. His little office, tucked away in a corner, was in a state of complete disorder and congestion, littered with unredeemed vouchers of un-returned books stuck on endless skewers rusting with age. Having lost all his money helping young artists with his books, the benevolent old man was now losing books to young students whom he was quite unable to chase up.

Until suitable rooms could be found for me, I continued very happily staying with the Bliss's, spending the evenings relaxed and at ease, and occasionally trying my luck on the piano, thanks to Mrs. Bliss's tolerance, when Douglas was out. When he was in, I remember him producing a number of Pre-Raphaelite reproductions, and we went through them together. The most I can say about the 'Brotherhood' is that they have excited my curiosity but never my feelings. They were self-conscious, and over-garrulous about art. In my time at the Slade aspects of art were not laboured. During the models' rests we might have discussed a particular point of interest but like as not little attention was paid to Wyndham Lewis' 'Blast', and generally we preferred kicking a tennis ball about in the Life Room. Wilkie, a fellow student, played for Chelsea, and we highly esteemed his skill. Any idea of a group of young artists bound together by theory was anathema to us. Lately an art historian from the Courtauld Institute pressed me to say what Henry Lamb, Stan and I talked about when on holiday as young men painting in Dorset. We anxiously awaited visits from H.G., as Henry referred to the Holy Ghost, but these visits were personal when they came and we struggled after our goals individually, 'finding the things that matter' each for ourselves. For the rest 'Art is 100 per cent living' as Stan said, and spirits were high. We were a group of friends, enjoying one another's company and stimulating each other to paint each according to his own conscience.

All the same in course of time 'groups' or 'schools' of painting do emerge. It is said that what is known as the 'Glasgow School' derived from the influence of the colour and tone of the top left-hand corner of Giorgione's 'Woman taken in Adultery' which hangs in the Glasgow Gallery—not the bottom right-hand corner which surely is an awkward bit of re-painting. The gallery certainly contains a most interesting collection, and there is plenty of good colour around. I liked the unusual way MacTaggert, the nineteenth-century R.A., mixed figures with landscape, as though he whipped them together like cream into butter. It was masterly too, how he tackled his 'Paps of Tura'; a photograph of him painting it shows him battling against the elements in a north-west gale, himself as well as his canvas caught up in a veritable web of guide ropes and both battened to the ground.

I soon lost any feeling that I was fighting a rear-guard action as I fell back on Glasgow, and by the time I moved to lodgings, in Kersland Street, just round the corner from the Bliss's I felt perfectly at home, and had made more friends. At parties (and those given by Mr. and Mrs. Beno Schottz were particularly happy occasions), I was introduced as a Sassenach to fellow Scots with the utmost caution.

Before I came to Glasgow, Dr. Honeyman, the keeper of the Art Gallery, had estimated to me that his idea of hell was Glasgow on a Sunday. Now I decided to see for myself what it was like, and walked the whole length of Maryhill Road, finally coming to rest in a wooden-seated coffee bar in Byers Road. A handful of decorative Glasgow girls were feeding juke boxes with coins in exchange for music, which I presume to them, far from echoing the torments of Dr. Honeyman's hell, sounded like the voices of the heavenly host.

I admit that there was nothing romantic about my room in Kersland Street, which was large and ugly, with clumsy furniture and fittings. But this was completely at variance with the delicacy and beauty of the ironwork in the Botanical gardens close by, a tribute to the skills of John Brown's foundry. One looked through the traceries as through a lace curtain, to the blue sky beyond. I spent many happy hours there marvelling at the sub-tropical plants, some of which grew in the open, reminding me of the nearness of the Gulf Stream, and that Glasgow is west of Land's End.

The heavier side of John Brown's skills burst upon me in the small hours of the morning, when roused from sleep, in a dazed and semi-shocked condition, I looked down on to the tram lines of Great Western Road as into a furnace at the shipyards. Men in strange helmets like hobgoblins, rushed around with acetylene welders which seemed to spark from them in every direction. Others in sub-human disguises armed with crocodile jaws wrenched great lengths of tram lines from the granite beds on which they had slept till judged outworn. By dawn, new ones had been flung down on the old foundations, and peace and quiet was restored as the hobgoblins disappeared into the belly of a monster lurking near by which carried them back to its daytime lair.

I spent part of my weekends round at the school where I did a long panoramic wash drawing of Glasgow from the 'Hen Run'. I also finished my picture 'The School on Peggy Hill, Ambleside' (now in the Kelvin Art Gallery), which I had brought with me. But I was missing my piano, and was indifferent about reading without Ursula, and started to occupy myself in my lodging house with an idea which had come to me when on holiday years before with our Balliol friends John and

Meg Campbell, on the Island of Canna in the Hebrides. At the time Meg was facing wild seas crossing to South Uist, where she was studying and transposing the subtle singing of the Islanders. There was no tape recording in those days, and she could only achieve this through the aid of her ear and knowledge of dialect. It was a help to her that we were able to put her in touch with Mr. Fox-Strangways on whom she made a deep impression. She made a deep impression too in quite another way on our daughter Gillian to whom she gave her earliest singing lessons. Proud father that I am, I cannot resist at this point taking another look at a well thumbed Royal Festival Hall Programme in which the name, Gillian Spencer, appears at the bottom of a dazzling cast in a concert performance of Figaro.

I myself at first seemed unable to make any progress with my painting while on the island. I always take a long time when breaking new ground, even at Grasmere, and Canna was far further afield and still more unlike my native countryside. I began to toy with an idea which emerged in my mind in the shape of a mural painting which was to include all that I associated with the island.

Meanwhile Meg suggested that I might like to draw an old woman living in one of the crofts. It was a dark and dingy little room in which I found her, and I was reminded of Millet's pictures and of Van Gogh's 'Potato Eaters'. Touchingly, she had smartened herself up for the occasion, but I could not help noticing her bundle of bedding piled up against the wall with a plate of fresh herrings resting on top of it, and above hanging on the wall, her rosary. When I had finished the drawing of her, she opened an old drawer, and pushing her gnarled hand into its darkest recess, dragged to the front, amidst various trinkets, several coins, exclaiming as she pushed them across the table to me 'Ach, I'm sure you ha' worked verra hard'. I took them, in spite of the strength of my anti-Roman tendencies, and on the way home dropped them into the offertory box of the R.C. Chapel.

It was a far cry to my ugly lodging in Glasgow from the romantic setting of that holiday long ago, and one would have expected any memory of it to have been banished out of sight and mind. But I was invited to contribute a painting to the 'Festival of Britain' and this prompted me to revive the idea I had had on my walks abroad on the island of Canna. Thus when Mrs. Patterson's daughter, Mary, had carried away my breakfast tray, I got out my drawing board and, shut in by the four walls of that most uninspiring large and tidy room in Kersland Street, I tried to come to terms with my 'Hebridean Memory' again. Looking at the drawing I made for it at the time it is surprising how successfully I got the off- and on-shore interchanges; yet all along I had thought of it in the terms of a mural painting, and I was using that technique against the far more complex requirements of an easel painting, and though I worked on it for three years, and it is one of the biggest canvases I have painted, it is now rolled up in my studio, and I look upon it as a sad failure.

Though the reason for this is evident to me, modern day psychology would no doubt put the blame, from the outset, on my landlady's daughter, Mary. Her solemn and silent entry each morning with my breakfast tray, and her re-appearance to fetch it away again acted like a damper on all my efforts. It was a lift to my spirits, and a pleasurable surprise, when observing what I was drawing, she asked me to put something in an autograph album for her. I drew a little girl about her age sitting on the ground. Behind her head like a halo I put a great red sun, and wrote above it something like 'May it shine for you'. For good measure I drew the head of one of those lovely Clydesdale horses which I had seen searching among the dustbins in Byers Road on their morning rounds. Once a dustman brought out some choice 'find' which he placed beneath the snuffling nose of the horse, and as he did so, looked up at me with a smile and winked.

I gave the autograph album back to Mary who received it without comment. This made me feel increasingly uncomfortable. The fear that I had offended her in some way began to haunt me. What could she have read into the drawings? Had I been too familiar? Were they suggestive in some way? She had a comely little figure, just the sort that would ripen to perfection one day, like the fine figure of a model whom I asked to sit for her portrait in my room at about the same time. A homesick Englishman, a master from another department at the Art School, asked if he could join me. He said Glasgow had had such a depressing effect on him that to get some relief he would go down to the Central Station every day to watch the 9.30 p.m. depart for Euston. What relief his effortless attempt at portrait painting could have possibly given him heaven only knew, and I began to wonder whether in fact he had merely been laid on as a chaperon by Bliss. In fact Mary's silence so unnerved me that I worked myself up to believe I was under suspicion in some way. Sooner or later the tangle had to be unravelled at its source. 'Mary!' I said at the next opportunity when she came to clear away my breakfast, 'Didn't you like the little drawing I did for your album?' As she turned away with my tray she replied 'It was for m'friend'. So much for the fears and fancies of a grass widower! But my days as such were happily numbered.

16

Culcreuch

1952

WHEN in November Ursula had paid a brief visit to me, Glasgow was in its worst mood. The cheerfulness of my letters, and welcome weekly cheques, and my regular comic letters to Gillian at school were in variance with her own assessment of the place, which was in keeping with that of Dr. Honeyman, and the poor homesick Englishman. Through the gloom and mist of Central Station as the train moved out I heard Ursula murmuring, 'It is a sort of hell, isn't it?' But it was not so for me.

I thought Glasgow at its best when blown all over the place by gale forces. Then was the time to get down to the Clyde, to see seals basking in a flurry of steam and sails, and to walk down narrow streets, rendered temporary cul-de-sacs by the towering bows of the *Queen Mary* in the basin of John Brown's shipyard. She seemed to be straining in the slipway to prove her sea-worthiness, and later, on a visit to the Jefferson Barnes' at Helensburgh, I had the opportunity to sit on the opposite bank, and watch her glide slowly down the Clyde on her first trials, sharing the gusts of sun and shadow as they swept up the river to Glasgow.

Had these experiences been Ursula's first introduction to Glasgow I might have been encouraged to go flat hunting sooner, but apart from the fact that there seemed none to be had, I was put off when the house that the new Head of the Design School had bought with Bliss's approval, proved to be all too perilously close to Glasgow's first line of defence against the Atlantic breakers. I also noted, by inference, that for me to go too far afield would not be altogether popular, as I would then be less easily available to deputize for the Director.

This I was soon required to do at Dumbarton where I had to address some sort of cultural society. The atmosphere at the meeting was an example of one side of the Scottish character, which can at times sit so heavily on the lighter flights of fancy or humour. No matter how hard I tried there was no response, and I returned to the home of my host in a state of deep depression, quickly dispelled by his inquiry: 'Well? did they look at you as though saying, "Interest us if you dare"?'

Soon after I was 'billed' to speak at Cambuslang. It was a town overshadowed by a great steel foundry, at that time only just recovering from the effects of the slump when grass had grown in the streets, and women had organized soup kitchens for the hungry. Now a man, who was standing at an open door appearing to be looking for somebody, accosted me when I thought I was lost, and assured me that this was the place where I was to speak, and brought me into a hall, empty but for a very few men. There were chairs on the platform, but no one occupying them, and I could not help feeling that the man who called me in was also whipping up passers-by to be my audience, as an odd one or two were added to our number. I suggested that the chairs be brought down from the platform on to the floor and we sat around together while I talked, till the much loved and looked for cup of tea emerged.

This was very different from my reception at Dumbarton, and I felt at home and in sympathy with those men, but the two evenings were enough to convince me that the less available I was to deputize as a speaker the better, and independently I began to inquire about flats outside Glasgow, in the hope that something might turn up to encourage Ursula to join me. She had little faith in my judgment in these matters—neither had I, so that when I rang her up and said I had the chance of a flat in Stirlingshire, she came north at once.

John Laurie, a member of the Staff, who with his wife was moving back to Glasgow, had whispered the magic name 'Culcreuth' in my ear, and he was kind enough to drive me over to meet Mrs. Menzies and to see the flat at the top of her house. One needs the pen of Scott to describe the wandering and unkempt drive of great length up which we drove, catching glimpses of the house which seemed to be gazing at us as it appeared and disappeared among the trees. At the time Mrs. Menzies was in a state of war with the British Army whose neglect in the upkeep of the drive she believed to have been a contributory cause to her husband's death. Returning home along the drive after dark he had been found dead—some said, frozen to death. This can happen in Scotland particularly at Culcreuch lying as it does at the foot of the Campsies, behind which the winter sun disappears soon after 3 p.m., producing an overwhelming and frightening darkness.

I would rather not dwell in memory on the fifty or sixty stone steps to our flat, but we were not worried by the long walk down the drive to the village of Fintry where we ran a perpetual and prosperous account in the only shop, kept by Mrs. Macnaughten. So anxious was she to oblige us in anything we asked that once at my request for braces, having searched high and low on the shelves, she disappeared behind scenes to return triumphantly with a pair which might well have belonged to her husband.

There were rather different shopping excursions with Mrs. Menzies when she shared taxis with us to Glasgow. This was for her the same as going to 'town' for English women, but the English are no match for Scottish ladies when it comes to 'turn out', and Mrs. Menzies' appearance was proof that Sauchiehall Street in Glasgow is every bit as fashionable as Bond Street.

There is no such comparison between villages in England and Fintry, which is little more than a slab of grey stone from roof down to the ground with no gardens. But though forbidding, we began to get the feel of it on our walks, and were not aware of any particular mistrust of us by the villagers. If they remained remote from us it was partly on account of their soft voices which made them almost inaudible to us as we passed. They would gather together in groups to talk, and one among them who particularly impressed us proved to be Sir Tom Johnston, Secretary of State for Scotland in Attlee's government.

He was not present at the meeting in support of the Fintry Labour candidate—but I was! At this election the Nenni Telegram took the place of the Zionist Letter in an earlier one, and I was not happy with the way those I judged to be the lairds were heckling the candidate about it. Daring to be a Daniel, I rose from my seat, and put one or two helpful questions to him which I thought he answered satisfactorily. In the silence that followed Mrs. Menzies, who was seated a few rows ahead of us, turned, and gave me a stern look, but she retained her seat, as did the candidate with a 10,000 majority!

The serious nature of Scottish education which starts at an early age was brought home to us by the children hastening to school their satchels stuffed with books of learning slung round their necks almost strangling them, and bouncing off and on to their little bottoms as they ran. We were invited by the schoolmistress to go and hear them sing, and the occasion became almost ceremonial. The children clearly regarded us as something very special, showing us to our chairs with the utmost formality, and singing to us in a solemn and dedicated way.

Once the bitterness of the dark winter nights was upon us we might see from our snug eerie the light of a hurricane lamp moving around on the fells above us, where perhaps a shepherd was fighting it out with the blizzard to save his sheep. These lowland experiences were Scotland for me, not Hogmanay, nor the much vaunted 'First Footing' on New Year's Eve, which was no more than carnal confusion, so that we were glad to wake up on New Year's Day to find ourselves still together. On the other hand to hear Archie Craig read 'Tam o' Shanter' (was it on Burns' Night?), was a revelation.

In the main we slipped back easily into the pattern of our winter evenings at Tree Cottage, Ursula reading, myself, drawing. There is nothing that gives me more inner confidence than a good drawing in the bag. Those drawings were the acme of challenge to me. I would prop up a mirror against some books and draw myself as I have loved to do ever since I entered the Slade. I was reminded of the continuing happiness and challenge these mirror drawings have brought me at every stage of my life when I received a letter from the Ashmolean the other day inquiring about a drawing of myself wearing a hat pushed to the very back of my head, dated February 9th, 1915. There in the photograph which they sent me was the hat, still after forty odd years, perched precariously on my head. I wonder where it had been, or rather how it had stayed on, all that time.

There were other drawings to delight me, for I illustrated books for Aldous Huxley and H. G. Wells and, as a result of a letter from Eiluned Lewis, an old friend of my wife's, I was asked by *Country Life* to illustrate her little book *In Country Places*. Among her gifts I noted a feeling for surrealism, as when she described a flood which washed the furniture, sofa and chairs downstream 'as well as a cabinet full of china which had come to rest on a bank with its contents unbroken'. I did an illustration of it at a perilous angle with a lovely vase exactly in the centre on top as though it was still at home, but the wallpaper had changed to a little country scene with willow trees and cows grazing, and the carpet to an eddying stream. How I enjoyed doing that drawing! I had the same experience illustrating a book of fables for Chatto & Windus by T. F. Powys. He was so pleased that the publishers bought one of the illustrations to give to him.

One reviewer asked why I was not employed as an illustrator more often, but the congested state of the dining-room table littered with my drawings would have given him an answer. However, it gave Ursula the excuse of indulging her love of what she called 'cosiness suppers' on the floor by the fire. I painted a portrait of her, which was a better painting than the one of the beautiful model in Glasgow, and a small canvas of the Campsies, both of which were building up my strength for a large painting from our window called 'Culcreuch' in which the happiness and homeliness of our life together again, after all the disappointments and setbacks, was reflected in what I saw and painted. It was as if south had come north and it was in this mood I decided to re-cross the border though not in person, by submitting this picture to the Summer Show at the Royal Academy.

I am rather pleased to have survived the whole of Sir Alfred Munning's Presidency as a successful outsider. Sir William Llewellyn's encouragement after my 'Cotswold Farm' success, and Connard's suggestion that my name should be placed on the candidate's list had as good as passed out of my mind with the passage of time, but on this occasion, instead of the usual form of acceptance for my picture, I received a telegram from Sir Walter Lamb telling me that I had been elected an Associate, and asking me for an immediate confirmation of my intention to be present at the banquet. I little thought when I signed my name on 'Culcreuch' I was as good as signing my resignation from the Glasgow School of Art.

17

Camberwell and 'The Scholar Gypsy' 1952–1958

I WAS sorry to leave Glasgow after only two years, but I realized that it was impossible for me conscientiously to fulfil a full time job and at the same time not to lose touch with my own painting. I slipped out with Ursula once for a long weekend to Derbyshire and back again with my master key through the side door. I do not know whether Bliss knew of my absence but I felt he would not like it. From the student's point of view I can think of nothing better than that a first class artist should be appointed to a school, but it must not be to the detriment of his own development. On the other hand one sympathizes with the principals of large and complex institutes who have to keep a fair balance between the advantages to the students, and the freedom of the artists. Subtle forms of abuse can arise, mostly I fear against the interests of the students. When I was at the R.C.A. I gave my whole time and attention to the Department for two full days a week. This could be argued to have been of greater value to the students than had I been on a full time basis with a studio on the premises.

As so often in life everything seems to happen at once. Shortly before receiving the telegram from the Academy, I had had a message from Leonard Daniels, the Principal of the Camberwell School of Arts and Crafts, asking me whether I would consider applying for the Head of the Department of Painting there. Leonard had been a pupil of mine at the R.C.A., and after the war had become a welcome neighbour and friend of ours whenever we were at Burdens. The salary he named was much reduced from that of Glasgow but I understood I would have more time for my own painting, and felt I would be happier now in the south. All in all the proposition looked so attractive, I applied for the post, and was appointed.

But first Stan and I were to converge on brother Percy's grand offices in Bedford Square to be rigged out for the Academy Banquet. One trusts there was a slight difference in our appearance from the evening, all those years before, when as boys we emerged from the Morrells' house, almost next door, togged up for the Opera in dress clothes sizes too large for us.

It was a fine evening so that we walked to Burlington House, and on the way Stan told me that my vote at the Election was one of the largest ever known – which I rather question. All the same forty-three ayes to five against was a remarkable volte-face from the Munnings period when, for want of support, there had even been a proposal to remove my name from the candidate's list. Now with Sir Gerald Kelly as the new President, and the winds of change blowing in my favour, there was a sudden change of heart among the members, and in spite of the declared secrecy of the ballot box, they followed their new President's wishes as faithfully as they had followed Sir Alfred Munnings during the whole of his Presidency.

I was summoned to appear before the Council to sign the Roll, and take the Oath, and was then directed by Sir Walter Lamb to cross the floor to be greeted by the President. He said very little, and his hand almost fell out of mine on to the table as we 'shook' hands. I was amused to be tipped off shortly after my election by Dame Laura Knight that 'Sir Gerald was a very dangerous man'. I was not on the Council with Kelly, not being eligible, but I did find favour with the next president, Sir Alfred Richardson, who told my wife, 'Take care of him, he's very good on the Council, and what's more he asks questions!'

With my A.R.A. and Camberwell in my pocket fortune seemed to be really smiling on me and mine, and we were off to a flying start when an invitation came from Lady Nicholls to spend a week at The Hague where her husband, Sir Philip Nicholls, was Ambassador. Lady Nicholls whom I had first known as Phyllis Spender Clay was, and remained always, a very real friend of mine since Garsington days.

Unlike my memories of docking at Southampton, arriving at the Hook of Holland had the same feeling for me as though *La Marguerite* was tying up alongside Bell Rope Meadow at home at Cookham. As we sped blissfully along in the Embassy car I thought of the little Gowans and Gray's picture books of those days, and of my present happiness to be about to see Dutch masterpieces in their own setting with Ursula and Gillian at my side.

We reached the Embassy just in time to change for dinner, but we experienced an anxious moment or two as we could not find our clothes, and there was much popping of heads out of doors by my wife and daughter looking along the passage, while I remained inside, as dignified as it is possible to be down to one's pants and vest, until a comely chambermaid entered bringing with her our clothes, beautifully pressed, and still warm from the iron, as she laid them out on our bed.

It was refreshing next morning to wake to see the Dutch getting off to work on their bicycles, their feet alone appearing and disappearing as they pushed and peddled on, and each bicycle so loaded that it was a wonder how they ever got on to them.

We entered the breakfast-room quietly, very quietly as the Ambassador and Phyllis were checking the day's engagements, reading from what at first sight appeared to be Bibles placed at their sides. If not the Ten Commandments, the pages were black with commands of a high order. Mixed in with calls to the Palace came 'The Spencers to Amsterdam' (Car) or 'the Spencers to Hitterlongon', and on one occasion to the opera. It was the only time I ever heard Kathleen Ferrier sing; nor had I heard 'Orpheus and Euridice' before. Dinner beforehand was formal, and for me conversation was strictly limited, as I was next to an Indonesian who had no English; but it was a delight to look across the table to see Gillian with her hair down to her shoulders, perfectly at home with the Dutch Foreign Secretary. Just before leaving for the opera we were alarmed to find her missing, and it was a relief when we got to our seats to see her already in place, having gone ahead with the First Secretary.

I am not particularly informed about pictures, and at the National Gallery have often liked to collect a chair and to join a group listening to a lecturer, particularly when he mixes in some homely details about the lives of the artists which can be so revealing. In Holland Phyllis sent us on a wonderful journey to the country to see a collection of Van Goghs—that happy earless genius. I say 'happy' because I feel about that desperate act, as about Mozart's pauper's grave, that surely geniuses such as they lived and died in heaven. In the brief period before his death, Mozart scored what are still regarded as his three greatest symphonies, and my brother in his last months could forget his pain working on his great unfinished canvas ('Christ preaching at Cookham') pinned to his bedroom wall.

Shortly after getting back from Holland I received a letter from County Hall instructing me to report there, I imagined to kiss hands on my appointment. In Glasgow my reception had been punctilious and dignified, not that I am suggesting that there was anything wrong about my arrival at County Hall, but it was different. I was shown into a room to be greeted by a nurse obviously carrying what my mother would have called 'a certain article' covered over with a cloth. Having followed the nurse's instructions I was able to return to her triumphantly in time to keep my appointment to lunch with Leonard at Camberwell. I did not tell him of my experience, but I wondered whether principals were treated in the same way at County Hall as heads of departments.

I had been told by Leonard that he had inherited a number of ex-service men and women who, on being demobbed, had opted to take up Art, and other kindred subjects. Their allowances were indeed lavish compared to my £16 in 1919, but by creating a situation which made life over-simple for them at first, too often discontent and disillusion followed after.

I tightened up the organization of the Department with some success among the students, but I soon gathered it was not so regarded elsewhere. Before taking my proposals to the office for typing, I had very properly taken them to the Principal to be agreed and signed. He initialed them without removing the sheet from my hand, and I suppose I could blame myself for not making them clearer to him, because, later, two members of my staff, who I imagined had come to discuss them with me, whiled away a few hours of their teaching time redrafting my notice, and it was their draft which replaced mine in all the classrooms.

The tempting original offer to be allowed to build up the Department as I wished, began to crumble yet further when I entered the Life Room to find two female models lying together on a mattress. I was put out by this, in fact I thought it sinister, but at the time I suggested in general terms that as most of the students could not yet cope with one model, let alone two, the Judgment of Paris was still a long way ahead of them.

In the end when I could bear no longer having the ground cut from under my feet, I followed the requirements of my appointment and wrote to County Hall for a clarification of the terms of my appointment.

I did not have to wait long before I was instructed to attend a meeting of the governors of the school with an ominous paragraph authorizing me to bring one friend with me. I did not expect anyone to 'keep the bridge with me', but I was not surprised to find the Principal and Chairman of the Governors awaiting me together with an L.C.C. Inspector and another 'High Up' from County Hall who was to chair the meeting. I rather liked the 'High Up'. Clearly he did not know how to begin, and the hesitancy of everyone looked like a stalemate until someone suggested that I had been absent. I rejected this, adding a little sharply 'How does anyone know?' This brought the Chairman of the Governors to life, protesting, and the 'High Up' from County Hall intervened to assure us that we were all getting on very nicely. 'You see Mr. Spencer' he said, 'you and I are of another generation', and then he took a half sheet of note-paper and wrote something on it which he passed over to me for my signature. It read, 'That Mr. Spencer agrees that the Principal should go round his Department'. I was so taken aback that I almost blurted out, 'But of course!' Instead I said I would be happier if it read, 'Mr. Spencer *welcomes* the Principal

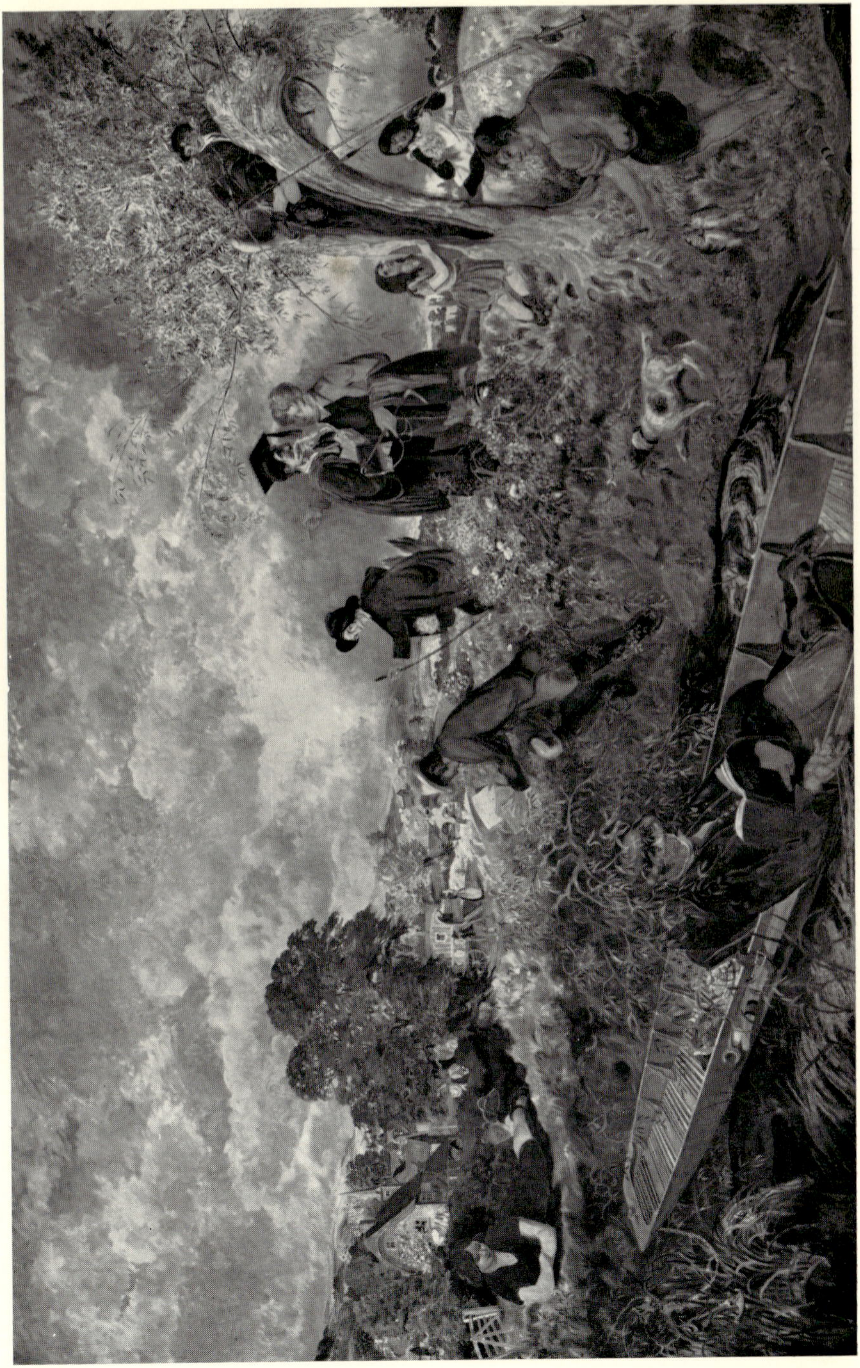

9 The Scholar Gypsy (1957)

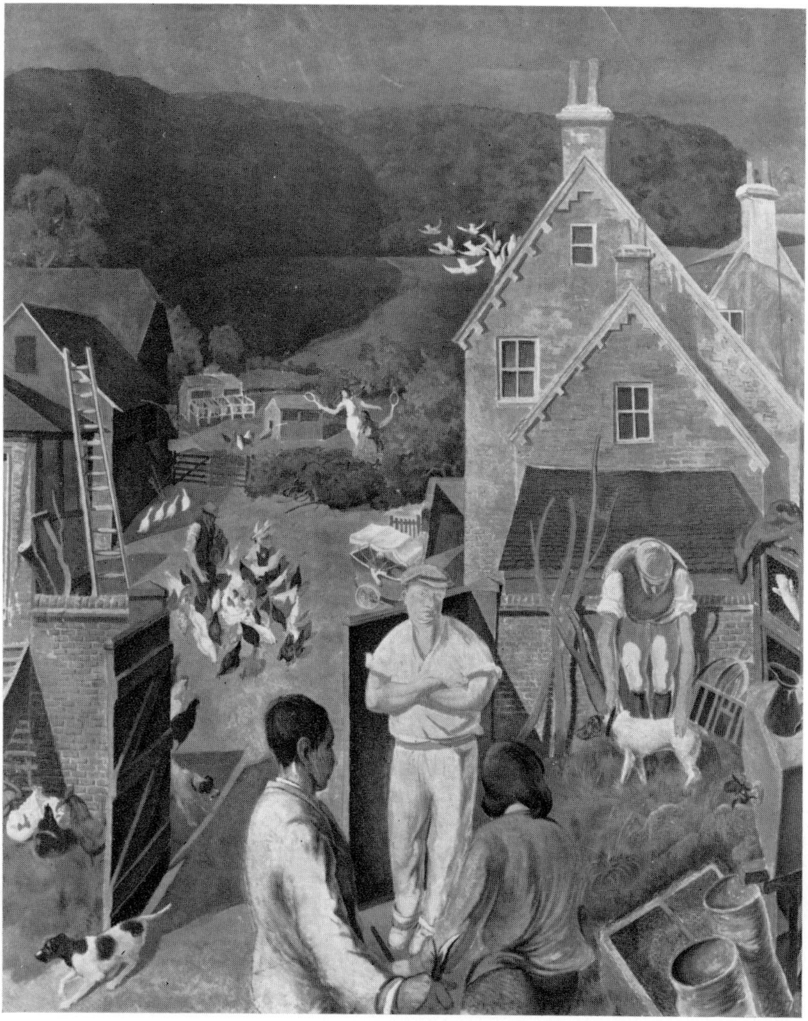

10 Hook End Farm (1957)

going round his Department at any time!' To this he would not agree leaving it to me to guess why. So I signed it as he had written it, the meeting closed, and I continued to direct the department in the interests of the students, with no backing from anyone, for the next four years.

As a teacher I would not describe myself as a traditionalist, for I did not mind if the students drew with their boots, if the result was good, but I preferred a good sharp B pencil. I never got on with charcoal, neither did Stan—it crumbled too easily at vital moments—though it was much in use at the Slade. I did not attempt to teach painting objectively, believing as my brother said of his first self-portrait at the foot of our bed 'It's all in the drawing', and this I taught by demonstrating in pencil on the side of students' boards. Some of these drawings of mine were good, others bad, but I never rubbed them out—for either way the pupil is heartened, and that is good teaching. I stressed the importance of surface appearances, rather than rules of anatomy or perspective, which can be destructive of feelings and ideas. I never forgot that I had received my own baptism in the middle of what has since been christened 'The Little Renaissance'. At the Slade the insistence was on grammar. For composition we were left to our own feelings, except for a monthly criticism by the masters. At the R.C.A. when I was teaching, there was generally a good spread of ideas hanging on the screens waiting for us in the lecture hall at the V. and A. Sometimes Rothenstein would take the criticism, and sometimes he would call on one or other of us to take it—today a student would be called upon—but there was general accord in those days between members of the staff, and few 'crossing of threads' which can only muddle, not widen, the horizons of the young.

Not long before the end of my time at Camberwell I was called to the Principal's room to meet Mr. Dalton, bringing to mind my own student days all those years ago when as Principal himself he had drawn a horse for me in indelible pencil. Equally indelible was my memory of him. His features were as refined as I had remembered, and now well over eighty years of age, he seemed a spirit from another sphere, while I still battled on unhappily earth bound. When I finally informed County Hall of my age I was not surprised that they replied with a curt note that they were regretfully unable to extend my services, though judging from names still remaining on the staff there up to the present they could have kept me on indefinitely had they wished.

* * *

While still at Camberwell I received a letter from the Abbey Trust inviting me to submit designs for three of the eleven arches in the arcading of the North Choir aisle of Lincoln Cathedral. I had long buoyed myself up in the hope that the Academy would make use of my services in the schools, for which I was fully equipped, but nothing emerged. Now I believe that the R.A. had moved at last. The letter fell as manna from heaven. In my excitement I failed to analyse it, but accepted it in good faith. I had just been reading Lady Burne-Jones's memoir of her husband in which she described Edward going to his study to 'ponder' a letter from the Dean proposing that he should paint the dome of St. Paul's!

I understood that it had been decided on a previous occasion that there should be a meeting between the Trust, the Cathedral Council, and those selected to paint the murals, to discuss subjects, and medium, such as whether canvas or board should be used. The meeting took place in London on January 20th 1953 at 4 p.m. As we sat down I noticed that there was nothing on the table at all except half sheets of note-paper headed 'Lincoln Cathedral Murals', and we had hardly settled in our seats before Mr. O'Rorke Dickey rose to explain that in the absence of any chairman he had been asked to tell us that the Lincoln murals were off! The Secretary, Mr. Blackmore, explained that the letter to that effect, which was not produced—perhaps its absence was the more revealing—had been received from Lincoln only that morning 'just in time'—just in time to have avoided a collision between maulsticks and crosiers! Finally Dickey turned to Duncan Grant and told him that the design he alone had already submitted, had been accepted. The meeting rose at 4.20 p.m.

As we were leaving, myself, for one, incredulous, Mr. Vincent Harris, who had been influential on the Abbey Trust for many years, assured me that other sites for murals would be found, and my hopes were again raised when soon after I received another letter to attend the offices to discuss plans for a mural in the University College Students Union which was then being built. The area was larger than that proposed for Lincoln, but the fee was far less, and I commented on this. This time Mr. Blackmore's explanation was that there had been certain 'difficulties' in agreeing Duncan Grant's fees at Lincoln, as the result of which they had decided to fix prices for the future at £3 per square foot as laid down by the Society of Mural Painters, and Mr. Harris, who seemed to have got out of bed the wrong side that morning, almost snapped at me that I could take it or leave it. It may have been some surprise to the meeting that I took it. But given such a chance to paint as this it was difficult to give much thought for the morrow.

Instead my mind became wholly absorbed in 'The Scholar Gypsy' which Ursula suggested should be the subject of my mural. The sound of her voice reading the poem to me stayed with me as I worked. At first it was I who walked down to the boathouse, and punted myself up-stream to Bablockhythe where I tied up alongside a bank scooped out by the water eddying and swirling into it at flood time; but then I felt I was Matthew Arnold himself who lay in the punt reading Glanville's book, his hand over the side, nonchalantly catching at some passing rushes. As the stern of the boat, happily for the design, swung out into the stream I swung out with it, glad to be able to go astern out of the picture, and to look back and view the scene as a whole, spotting 'The Scholar Gypsy', as he passed across the meadows towards the woods, and Clough on the bank above his friend, his mind running with the lines about the struggle being so worthwhile. Certainly I found my own struggles with the eddying water and that punt wholly worthwhile, not to say joyous. The wall I had to cover came slap down to the ground, so I lay flat on the floor, painting straight from memory, and building up my whole mural upon it. No one, not even Stan, could have painted the punt better, in fact some of his punts in 'Christ preaching at Cookham' are rather clumsy. Mine was the keystone to the whole picture which depended not only on the mood of the poem, but on intimate knowledge. I knew well and could share with Arnold all that was happening in the picture. The boy up the tree was myself; the boy with the fishing rod could have been myself, or my friend Frank Godfrey. But I overlooked, perhaps excusably, the feelings of the undergraduettes! Though my designs were accepted with acclamation, the Students Committee came up with that one objection. Happily I was able to put it right by sending a gypsy resting under a tree back to her caravan, and painting an undergraduette in her place, though she had left her cap and gown behind, and was watching a water rat swimming for dear life from a dog snuffling along the bank.

All was now in the clear, or so I thought, and I was off almost the next day to report to the Clerk of the Works, and get my cards which I barely looked at, beyond stamping, prepared to live again the happiness I had experienced at Holywell Manor. I repeat it would have been folly to be wise given the chance to paint that mural, but the fact remains that in the course of the next two years while I worked on my 'Scholar Gypsy', catching the train at crack of dawn from Reading and wending my way home at night, I had used up all the £460 that I was paid for the work, and was forced to flog more and more of the value of my house to the bank, until I feared there would be no house left.

I described my situation to the Secretary of the Academy, who passed it on to the President, Sir Charles Wheeler, who in his turn invited me to join him for coffee, after lunch, at the Athenaeum. The result of our meeting was that I was commissioned to paint a large decorative mural for the R.A. Restaurant under the Leighton Fund for £1,000. I was disappointed that my proposal that I should join the staff of the Painting School was not taken up, as I should have been thankful to rest awhile after my 'Scholar Gypsy', but finance was the driving force, and I began my task. It was an eighteen-footer with the title of 'An Artist's Progress', nearly a pot boiler, but I found quite a lot to interest me in it. It was, of course, my own progress from Cookham to the Slade, and finally to the Academy where on the extreme right of the wall I painted myself entering the council room to sign the Roll on my election. I took a friend to see it recently and noticed that, innocently enough I think at the time, I had left my painting kit, which had been inseparable from me during the whole of my 'progress', outside the door of the Council, wherein one might point a moral!

I have said it was a near-miss to a pot boiler, but after all it had been given to me to keep the pot boiling. However as time went on I began to wonder if it was not also intended to shut me up. In the end I decided to write to Mr. Blackmore, who as far as I knew was still the Secretary to the Abbey Trust, to ask him to let me see the files about the University College Commission. To my surprise the reply came from Mr. Sidney Hutchinson, the librarian at the Academy, who told me that Mr. Blackmore had had a stroke and been 'bundled off' to the Isle of Wight, and that he, Mr. Hutchinson, had now taken over the secretaryship to the Abbey Trust. He had hunted through trunks and boxes of papers but he could find no files on any business before 1960. There then followed an extremely lengthy correspondence between the President and myself, which seeing that none of the papers of deep concern to me were accessible, was completely unavailing. My only gain was when he wrote that he had gone through Blackmore's papers, and had found them 'not very helpful'. At least he must have been aware of their wholesale destruction.

The affair was so disturbing that there seemed nothing left for me but to write and tender my resignation. The President replied that it had been received with great surprise by the Council, who would like further information than was contained in my 'laconic' note. This was rather strange after all the correspondence that had passed between us, some of which should surely have come before the Council, but I set to work and drafted a full report of 3,000 words built out of our correspondence, and after a lull received the following letter from the Secretary to the Academy, Mr. Humphrey Brooke:

Dear Mr. Spencer,

I have been asked by the President and Council to express to you their thanks for the extreme care with which you have put down the facts concerning your dispute with the 'Abbey Memorial Trust'.

The President and Council share your view that artists commissioned by this committee should be paid a properly negotiated fee appropriate to highly gifted artists. They know, however, that this is now the practice of the Committee. Certainly since 1960 when our Librarian became Secretary there has been no case in which an artist has been dissatisfied with his fee. It is also significant that the Society of Mural Painters no longer use a recommended scale of payment.

The President and Council regret that at one time as evidence by Mr. Blackmore's letter of January 4th 1957 the Committee appears to have adopted a scale then laid down by the Society of Mural Painters. They entirely agree with your view that artists of repute should not be rewarded on a basis of so many square feet.

If this Committee should ever again adopt a similar procedure they trust that any future Presidents and Council would take effective action under the powers vested in them for the variation of the Academy's representation on the Committee.

A copy of this letter is being sent to the Secretary of the Abbey Trust, and it is hoped that you will find its terms a sufficiently unequivocal assurance.

I withdrew my resignation not with much assurance that Trusts are always to be trusted, or their terms always respected, but at least with the satisfaction of having brought off 'The Scholar Gypsy' by hook or by crook. Unlike Mr. Bratby in a recent letter to *The Times* complaining about V.A.T. on art, I do not believe that artists should be, or ever have been, protected from worry, financial or otherwise. Mr. Bratby even expressed concern as to how V.A.T. might have affected Beethoven or Van Gogh, but Van Gogh barely sold a picture in his lifetime, and Beethoven's art rose above every affliction including law suits, war, and physical handicap.

An intriguing footnote to my 'Scholar Gypsy' is that the two walls at the Students Union, on the staircase above my mural were offered to my brother. Unknown to me he came to see my work, and wrote to the Martineaus 'Gilbert's lovely painting in the Students Union is a magnificent figure composition, but there is plenty of lovely landscape. My compositions are in steep perspective so that there is little or no landscape.' However, to the Warden he said that he 'would show Gil how to do it!' All he said to me was that of course the fee was ridiculous, and that if he did it he would regard the payment as 'expenses', and the murals, as a gift, and in some ways the chance to paint a mural would have been as much a gift to him as to the Nation. It is tantalizing to think of what might have regaled University College students for all time, had he not died. In the event two designs by Sir Thomas Monington decorate the walls.

18

No Remorse

1958–1964

WITH Camberwell, 'The Scholar Gypsy' and the 'Artist's Progress' all behind me I was quick to switch back to the fodder I had collected on my walks at Upper Basildon, and to look again at my notes and ideas. Three pictures kept edging their way in with the titles 'Summer Evening, Durdham Downs', 'Summer Evening, Burden's Farm', and 'Summer Evening, Hook End Farm' in which I played light figures against a darkening background. In this I was influenced by Henry Lamb's Manchester War picture, and another of newspaper boys with their bicycles outside Poole Station. But the job for me was to find valid reaction of my own to the notion. It was not a simple case of putting light figures against dark backgrounds, but of dealing in 'Summer Evening, Hook End Farm' with a double viewpoint. Walking down from Hare Green with Ursula we first saw the farm, as I have painted it with the dark Hook End woods rising behind. By the time we had dropped down to talk to the farmer, Mr. Ambler, my viewpoint had changed, see-saw fashion, and I was able to get the best of both worlds.

I am satisfied that this picture for me was some kind of a breakthrough. I painted it on the sofa in our drawing-room with Ursula reading by the fire, able, if I wished, to go over to the piano and have another go at some of the less intractable classics. This freedom to mix my interests and work without restraint is not possible in portraiture when 'finding the thing that matters' as Henry Lamb put it, while the sitter sits hopefully, is a strain. Though I have brought off some good ones, I have always preferred to search for 'the thing that matters' in a composition of my own at my own pace and to have time to ponder over points in my pictures.

Besides my 'Summer Evening' farm pictures, I painted another farm, 'Brook Farm' in Suffolk, in the late summer of '58 for which Henry Lamb, whose praise was not easy to come by, gave me marks. We met by chance in the Kardomah Café on the day of the Private View of the Academy the following spring, but his praise reminded me of overhearing him and Stan many springs ago agreeing on the other side of the hedge that I would never be a good painter because I was too healthy! This must have rankled with me as I had always remembered it. He, of course, had forgotten all about it, but I rather enjoyed reminding him of it when in explanation of my successful painting I said, 'You see, Henry, I haven't been feeling very well lately!'

Somehow in spite of the dubious advantage of good health I managed through various ways and means to carry on over this lean period. There were occasional interventions from painting which I much enjoyed when I taught at summer schools at Bigwood or Flatford. There was a lovely little tea garden in the village of Flatford where we used to sit in a veritable fog of talk and theories. Nor were the summer schools just for fun only. Some of the 'students' had been trained in their younger days and could be taken seriously; others were preparing their palates for more important painting to come, so that the final criticisms of their work often required a lengthy and searching analysis.

At Bigwood I ran up against pure genius in the person of an elderly lady who was churning up paint in a spirit of intense enthusiasm. Pointing at a little bare patch of canvas which I assumed was meant to be the sky showing through the trees she exclaimed passionately, 'Mr. Spencer, Mr. Spencer, is that *all right*?' 'Yes', I said, 'I think so', to which she replied, 'I am so glad, I am *so* glad. I left it there for the birds to fly through'.

I remember returning to Tree Cottage, and recounting this experience to Ursula, who was very amused. It was then that she told me that she had arranged to go into Reading Hospital for a check-up. I had to go away again, but she took herself off to the hospital quite simply on the 'bus, and when next I saw her, she was moving about the ward talking to patients, and spoke especially affectionately of a little coloured nurse. I was called away to go to see the house surgeon whose brother had been a pupil of mine at Camberwell. Now he told me of the sinister nature of Ursula's trouble and that he could offer me no hope of her recovery.

After the operation, she barely recovered consciousness. Gillian and I sat on either side of her each of us holding a hand. Stan arrived, and I remember the Sister coming in while he was there and touching me on the shoulder. I was momentarily overcome, and to my surprise he remarked quickly, 'It's a pity there isn't more of that.' When he left he said, 'You needn't worry about her any more.' Both remarks were strengthening.

I had no difficulty in planning Ursula's service, as

we had from time to time discussed and agreed what we felt about death and burial in the abstract. Thus I kept it as impersonal as possible, but the large assembly who crowded about Gillian and me and greeted us when we came out of the chapel made us happy and proud. I know what I meant when I said to one of our friends, 'This is a triumph.'

Gillian returned to London and I to Tree Cottage. All on my own I took Ursula's and my favourite walk to Hare Green carrying the little box containing her ashes which I scattered there. The two little Peckham girls were playing around as usual at their cottage gate. Shortly afterwards on one of my walks I met a very old friend and neighbour, Mrs. Messenger, who tapped me on the shoulder and said, 'Remember, no remorse!'

It was Ursula's great strength that made it possible for me to stand up to her absence as though she were still there. I knew we had been of the same mind about life and death which somehow made it less difficult when it was left to me to put it to the test. Still I was almost taken aback by my own resilience which she herself had remarked on just before she went into hospital. Her last message to reach me came from the Sister, who told me that Ursula had said just before the operation, 'I have had a happy life.' Stan who was within a few months of his own death wrote, 'Art is a kind of searching for home and Ursula would, I feel, be with me if I say it still is to be sought and found.'

Now my first step in my search for home again was to ask Joffre Evans whether he thought his wife would give me a helping hand. He answered, 'You can ask Joyce, Mr. Spencer, and if she says "Yes", that will be all right with me'. She was still helping me when eleven years later I packed up Tree Cottage to go to Walsham-le-Willows. Just before she came to me I greatly appreciated the elder Mrs. Evans's invitation to lunch on Sundays at 'Willowdene' as it gave me a chance to draw her, which I had always wanted to do. It was hung on the line at the R.A. in 1960 and now hangs at Willowdene.

Other helpful occupational therapy came my way in what I called 'commissions at risk' from my friends and neighbours so that I was soon out and about as usual, finding subjects to paint and draw. What I have called the 'breakthrough' in my painting was coming along well, and continued after Ursula's death, helping to bridge the time between 'before' and 'after'.

The piano had always taken the place for me of reading in the evenings, and I now reinforced the habit by keeping a log of how long it took me to get through what I was playing. Thus I see recorded on the flyleaf of Vol. I of Mozart's sonatas that on January 21st 1964 I played without repeats between 9 p.m. and 10.45 p.m. the sonata in E flat K282 and Beethoven's Opus 2, No. 1 in F Minor. Gerald Finzi and Gillian showed me how to play those teasing first bars in the Mozart. There was a family dictum that if one could not play presto with the right notes, then for God's sake treat it as an adagio until you could. The finale of Haydn's Sonata No. 5 in C kept me happy for evenings, but I no longer had Ursula's encouragement as she sat by the fire with her book, 'You are playing rather nicely tonight, darling'.

Once a man in the Red Lion told me he wished he could play the piano, and I advised him not to do exercises, but to play! By this method, in my own way, I have played through most of Mozart and Haydn sonatas, and some Beethoven. At one time Stan and I were each taught a Beethoven sonata by Mrs. Harter, a pupil of Kathleen Long. I don't know how Stan fared, but I fell by the wayside and returned to my old wicked ways, and lived.

I now began to enlarge my reading, extending it beyond *The Oxford Book of English Verse*, which had always been my Desert Island choice, to Wordsworth's 'Prelude'. I stood up to read it, but found the silence disturbed my concentration, and to correct this took to reading it aloud.

Only six months after Ursula's death, Stan died. He died, not unexpectedly in the Canadian Hospital at Cliveden, where Ursula and I had both visited him after his first operation. Then, propped up on the pillow behind him, was a half finished drawing of a nurse, and he said he meant to do another one if he had half a chance. He did have half a chance, and courageously continued painting his 'Christ preaching at Cookham Regatta', pinned up on his bedroom wall both at the vicarage and at Fernley. But by October news reached me that he was back in Cliveden Hospital again. This time I visited him with Gillian. He had his Doctor's hood and gown which he had just received from Southampton University beside him, and she leant over his bed and he put it on her.

Cookham on the day of his funeral had something of the feeling of the regatta about it. There were no flags of course, but Crowds! Police! Traffic! Muffled Bells! and as we turned round Bridge Corner to enter the churchyard, those hydraheaded monsters, the B.B.C. arc lights were leering and glaring down the path to the porch. How unreal it all seemed! I lost Percy and Pamela as we entered the church, but Gillian and I found ourselves taken over by an usher who led us up to a front pew, only to find Dudley Tooth seated at the other end. I don't know what his feelings were. We did not speak, and after the Service he left by the south aisle and Gillian and I by the nave.

Lord Astor's address redeemed by its simplicity some of the awful and bewildering preparations going on outside. I congratulated him on his reference to my brother as a 'buttress', not a pillar, of the Church. This he told me he had got from Winston Churchill whose subtleties in the use of words were so masterly. But my mind kept on wandering. How unlike this was to anything that belonged to one's memories, and yet I could not help thinking that, had Stan been present, he would have brushed aside all such sentiments and repeated his walk up to Cookham Station, and back, curious to see what people would say! I thought too of my father's funeral. Then Percy and I were the sole mourners following the hearse. No one else came. Having ordered two cabs, to give something of a ceremonial appearance, we put the undertakers into the spare one, and thus left the village with Father, for the last time, on the way to the cemetery. But as we turned beneath Cannon Down Bridge the hearse was struck by a car which sent it sideways across a low hedge, happily without upsetting it. The car ricocheted off on to the cab containing the undertakers who issued out of it like a swarm of bees. The chauffeur, sheepishly wiping the peak of his hat, explained that he was baring his head and momentarily lost control of the wheel. For sheer presence of mind I suggested to Percy that we should tip him! Unfortunately his story did not save him from the Maidenhead Police Court and his share in my father's funeral was a £10 fine.

After Stan's death naturally there were many inquiries and letters, one from an old friend Victor Gollancz (Stan and I were at his wedding), asking me to go and see him. When I went he outlined the sort of book he would like me to write about Stan. I knew he had already been in touch with him about publishing a biography, and they had even discussed an author, but already Collins had crossed the thread, by lining up Lord Astor's protégé, Mr. Collis, to write a life, so it was important my book should get in first if it was to get good publicity. I told Victor what I thought I could do, and the shape it might take, as some time before I had written an account of early life at Cookham which had got lost in my many moves before settling at Basildon. Fortunately, I still had the notes I had made for it, and I suggested I could build up what I called a backcloth to Stan's life from them. Victor remained silent for a moment puffing at his cigar, and then said, 'Yes, I think you're right' and advanced me £200 over and above the contract to get me going.

Sometime before my brother's death, when he was still vigorous but dying, I visited him at Cookham Vicarage where he was being looked after by Mrs. Westropp. He said he was prepared to take on a bet with me that 'they will get that man Collis to write my life'. He would have won his bet. He had only met him at the very end of his life while painting Lord Astor's portrait at Cliveden. Collis had been in semi-residence there writing a little memoir of Nancy, Lady Astor. At home, all we knew of Lady Astor was that her husband was a retiring man of simple habits, whose father, so we were told, 'built New York!' When people scoffed at his waiting for his small change at the toll gate on Cookham bridge, my father always stoutly defended him.

It so happened that at the time of writing my book I was staying with the Martineaus, close friends of Stan, and neighbours of Lord Astor. They had been asked to dinner at Cliveden to meet Collis; Jack Martineau, being one of Stan's trustees, and I went along with them. Among the guests was John Rothenstein whom we had known almost since his childhood, and one could not but wonder how Collis's name had been introduced as Stan's biographer, when there were people like John in touch with the family, and well placed to gather first hand information from those of us, brothers and sister, still alive and not always uncritical, in the strongest position to give help. Consequently I was a little surprised when Collis's only remark to me was, 'All I want from you is a few dates'. The misgivings I felt then for the book he was to write were vindicated a couple of years later.

Meanwhile the publication of my own book, *Stanley Spencer, by his Brother Gilbert*, was well timed, and gave me the largest press I have ever had. I was staying at the 'Folly Arms' Hotel at Torrington at the time having been commissioned by the Hereford Art Gallery to paint two landscapes for them, and I became quite an object of interest not only on account of my paintings, but for the state of my breakfast table each morning when I never knew whether I was cutting through my bacon and eggs or a wad of press cuttings.

From this time on many questions and conundrums about my brother's works have naturally come my way, and I have had to be on my guard. One afternoon returning to Tree Cottage I received a telephone call from a gentleman who told me he was speaking from Burghclere and was a great lover of my brother's pictures. He asked could he come over and see me on his way home to London. I was delighted he should do so, but when he arrived his appearance did not impress me, and in the course of our conversation he explained that he had a four-foot canvas in his car which he was convinced was an authentic work by my brother. It was clever, I thought, but a bit too clever. It appeared to be painted latterly when I knew that my brother painted some of his worst pictures. All that my visitor could tell me was that he had bought it from an antique dealer in the West Country. I had to be circumspect as I knew a provenance from me would be valuable, so when I later saw it reproduced as being by my brother in a brochure of an important London agency, I pointed out, through my solicitor, what had happened, and why I had my doubts. This lover of my brother's art now returned to me in a very different mood. I remember phrases such as 'queering his pitch' and how he had already 'sold a half share in it'. Joyce, who was in the kitchen at the time, said it sounded as though we were having a free fight.

On another occasion I was visited by a jockey from nearby Compton, who wanted me to help with a thesis he was preparing about my brother. Whether, taking the long view, he was covering himself against not winning a Derby, I did not ask. After giving him tea, I got down my Phaidon book (*Stanley Spencer* by Elizabeth Rothenstein) and other photographs of my brother's work and talked about the pictures much in the same way as my brother would have gladly talked to him about them. Before he went, I said that as I had helped him, he might help me in return, and I showed him a little picture of a string of horses exercising on the Downs. How I enjoyed those horses! Ursula and I often came on them on our walks behind Compton, the trainer, riding bareback on a pony, watching them. Naturally the picture had leanings towards impressionism, but I had looked closely for characteristics as to loose or tight reins, long or short stirrups. My visitor said that one of my stable lads had such a short stirrup he was fancying himself as a future Lester

Piggott. Encouraged by his interest, I sent my picture to the R.A. and sold it at the Private View.

I do not know whether in the end my friend rode in the Derby, or went to Reading University, but his visit reminded me of the Reading Art Gallery which was about to open its doors to me. In the old days, it was not only overshadowed by Silchester as a collection, but hopelessly overwhelmed by the enthusiasm of the Chairman, Dr. Hurry, for the history of Reading. This took the form of his presenting periodically vast canvases of historical events which were so bad that it was said the previous Director's state of mind reached a condition of neurosis when the sound of trolley wheels on the flagstones below signalled the arrival of yet another historical scene. Looking at one of these, one felt that the 'Abbey' could just as well have fallen right down while it was about it. As to 'Summer is a cummin in' far better, had it never come into the gallery at all!

Since the death of Dr. Hurry, and other changes, the Reading Art Gallery had had a considerable face lift, and I was gratified in 1963 to receive a letter from the Director inviting me to hold a retrospective exhibition there, and suggesting I should get in touch with Dr. Sheila Percival.

Accordingly I arrived at the gallery, but not knowing where to go, approached a young lady and asked her whether she could tell me where Dr. Percival could be found. 'But I am Dr. Percival', she explained. I was so delighted, and relieved that I promptly took her out to lunch at the 'Coach and Horses'. Our conversation ranged over various aspects of the exhibition, but I had very little difficulty in arriving at a title for it. To Dr. Percival's suggestion 'A Retrospective Exhibition', I answered firmly, 'No! "*The*" '. Now, ten years later, that I am being offered a retrospective exhibition by the

Fine Art Gallery, I still dwell affectionately on *The* Retrospective Exhibition at Reading, and can never be grateful enough to the Director, Mr. Gwatkin, and Dr. Percival for the trouble they took. In the beginning they tore the guts out of a single decker 'bus, filled it with racks of pictures, instead of passengers, and chased all over the country for them, with nothing more to guide them than my memory. By the end my every wish had been fulfilled. No formal opening, no party, no drinks, best of all no price lists! But Dr. Percival who was most solicitous about my interests in case there were any 'inquiries' dotted a few prices down on a sheet of paper, which I think she placed between two sheets of blotting paper on her desk. There was no whisper of this in the gallery, but it had the effect of the Chapati in the Indian Mutiny so that I remember her murmuring to me, 'You are going to become a rich man'. It was timely indeed, and helped me to recover from my disastrous adventures in the Abbey Trust jungle.

I do not forget that it was the town, not the gown, that did me honour in Reading. The Deputy Mayor and Mayoress were early arrivals at the Private View, followed by a policeman. This gave just the note we Spencers liked. Perhaps I also had, in miniature, Stan's feelings when he was awarded the C.B.E. and walked up to the station and back to see 'what people would say', I now saw with pride that the Reading buses carried sticker labels on their sides advertising my exhibition, and the local press, too, did me proud.

It is not for me to form other people's judgments of the exhibition. Naturally I was very anxious beforehand as I had painted some of the pictures fifty years earlier and others merely a matter of months before. The general effect on me was one of happiness that there was from first to last a reiteration of my feelings and evidence of my Slade training throughout. In spite of the years between them, these pictures, even the ones I had forgotten, seemed to have kept alongside me.

It might be thought that in these changing times I had not sufficiently changed. My own hope is to have developed? but to have kept my roots. I have visited France, Holland, and Italy to see the paintings of those who also stayed at home, not to learn, but to love. I like Cézanne for saying, 'Why should I leave my own doorstep?' Deliberate obscurantism has no place with me, and surely the visual common ground which best conveys a message must be respected.

I wished that Stan could have been present at my exhibition. He would have met so many of our old friends, away from his more recent influences, and I should have liked to hear him say again, 'Gil doesn't know how good he is'. For here was an early little composition in wash on paper made in 1915 of the 'Ascension' 20½ inches x 20½ inches (Mrs. Gerald Finzi) and another of the same period of the 'Descent' (19 inches x 19 inches) belonging to Bob Gathorne-Hardy which Stan so much admired that he had positively bullied me into trying to resolve it into a full blown painting after the war. Never did I sacrifice a fine composition to a greater act of folly. I sent the result to the academy where Stan looked at it without comment, and I tore it to ribbons with a razor the minute the exhibition closed. However that was not the end of the story for I borrowed the original drawing from Bob Gathorne-Hardy and had another shot at it, painting it in oil on paper to my complete satisfaction. I imagined how Stan seeing it would have turned to me with his characteristic, 'Well, of course!' meaning of course he had been right that the little composition for the 'Descent' was good and why had I not in my first attempt struck to the original drawing, as was his absolute rule.

The truth is that when I made the original drawing I was young and uncomplicated, and had complete confidence in what I drew. Without this matter of fact directness of approach, the stuffing is knocked out of religious paintings. I used to say to Ursula that had I the faith of a fundamentalist like our grocer, whose beliefs were as solid as the goods in his basket, what pictures could I not have painted. But Stan was not worried by personal religion. By relating the life of Christ to everyday life in Cookham, he was able to remain on his own ground. Moreover, he wrote that he felt a religious picture was 'not necessarily a painting having a specific religious subject, but something where you felt its presence', and he found that presence in Cookham.

Once he had written to me, 'Cookham was for you, as it was for me. We both of us had identical sympathies, but a different sort of approach.' For his exhibition in Cookham Church he wrote, 'While I have a certain respect for my landscapes I was never able to express in this form the meaning that was to be found in Cookham. It was when I painted what I had imagined that I came nearer to the feeling that Cookham gave me'. Now, surrounded as I was at my retrospective exhibition with landscapes such as 'Sashes Meadow' spelling out my love for the Berkshire countryside, our 'different sort of approach' was made manifest. Yet our 'identical sympathies' for Cookham remained constant. Crossing from his exhibition in the church in 1958 we walked together for the first time round the vicarage gardens, and saw an aspect of the village we had never seen before. Stan's solitary comment, 'Mysterious!' immediately and forcibly echoed my own feeling. Here, in this view hidden from us for so long, was evidence of the strange magic Cookham still held for us.

In fact so sensible am I of our shared experiences and inheritance, from which Stan's inspiration sprang, that, though a little burdened with a sense of my responsibility, I will try to set down in the next chapter some of my own reactions to his life and work.

19

Stan

THE late Mr. Eric Newton in his review* of my book, written in 1961, wrote, 'Gilbert and Stanley Spencer were more than brothers, they were affinities! A special key is needed for an acceptance of the deeper levels of Stanley's art and that Gilbert possesses almost unconsciously.' But the key did not belong to me alone. The whole family possessed it. Stan, as I have often claimed before, could not have been more fortunate in his parents and home as a backcloth to all that followed. Not that we regarded our way of life as unusual. We knew no other, so had no means of judging. But the concentrated thought and interests which surrounded us as children almost inevitably took root in us as we developed. Stan at one time, in his peculiarly inverted vanity, preferred to put about the 'Peasant Stock' idea of his origin, playing the part of 'village boy makes good'. Only in his last years did he write, 'I have to admit that in my family surroundings I was not the only pebble to be found in the shingly stream down Odney', and Henry Lamb, finding us all sitting round having tea, commented in his quiet voice to Darcy Japp whom he had brought to meet us, 'In my Father's house are many mansions'. It is true that we were totally unconcerned where we came from, and happily oblivious where we were going either. Once, at dinner, my father told us that we had come over from France

* *See Appendix.*

with the Dispensers, a lot of scoundrels, who, he explained, no doubt in deference to the common decencies of mealtimes, had put out the 'eyes' of Edward II with a red-hot poker. Over and above this I have recently discovered that our great-grandmother's name was appropriately 'Riddle'. Perhaps therein lies the answer to my father's impressive mental powers, and musical gift, far in advance of those of a normal villager. Sir George Young, a cantankerous, critical sort of man, appointed my father to tutor his son Hylton in the classics during his vacations from Cambridge, and said that the Spencers must have descended from a long line of something extraordinary.

Lately I came on a letter written by my father to my brother Sydney in July 1918 (the last letter he can have received before he was killed), in which my father adds in the postscript 'During the last fortnight I have nearly got through the *Aeneid* without a crib, and pretty well I think. I do so enjoy it!' This was the same man of whom Sydney records in his diary, 'Father gave me nearly two hours of a piano lesson, one of the cleverest he has ever given me. I felt as though I had been pulled through a hedge backwards when he had finished with me!' Apart from music there are frequent accounts of the interest he excited in us all in literature, astronomy, botany or bird life. As he 'bolted' to and from his organ loft at Hedsor he would notice the habits of a dab-chick, or crossing London Bridge, watch 'the fascinating flight of sea gulls', and in another of his letters he describes how he led us off 'down to the Churchyards to hear the owl's snore. After a long time Gil clapped his hands and then a beautiful fluffy thing fluttered down through the twilight. It landed at my feet, a snowy-white owl with brown wings. I put my hat over it, and Stan carefully picked it up, and carried it to the village to show it to anyone who would like to see it. We then carried it back and Stan carefully threw it up into the fork of the tree'. This reminds me of the feeling that Stan got into his picture of Christ in the Wilderness tenderly holding the scorpion.

There were innumerable walks, 'up the strand over Widbrook', 'down Odney', 'up Cockmarsh', and uphill or downhill the talk kept pace. On a special day when Will was home on holiday Sydney wrote, 'After breakfast Will, Percy, Father, Gil, Stan and I went for a walk over the fields up Rowborough, along the top of Barley Hill, and so to Cockmarsh where we saw the first swallows'. Talk ranged from a discussion on majority rule to the effect of the eclipse which reminded Father of Tennyson's lines in the Idylls, 'He drew himself bright from his old dark life'. 'In the afternoon Gil, Stan and I had Will to play Beethoven to us from two till 3.30.'

In such company Stan did not lack for stimulation, but one might ponder how his genius would have developed had there been enough money to send him to a conventional school, or what, had he studied under Stanhope Forbes, which was seriously considered, that kindly man would have made of him. We were naturally obedient and respectful towards any one who taught us, and ready to work hard on the lines laid down for us. No student at the Slade did his work more thoroughly than Stan or left more of it lying on the floor to be swept up by Mrs. Kauffman, the charlady.

Until Stan began coming home from the Slade, his pockets stuffed with Gowans and Gray's Old Master Series, painting was the one subject which had not naturally cropped up in family talk. The discovery of the Italian primitives, and the impression they made on him, entered into him like some kind of stigmata. There was nothing sensational in this as in the conversions we were accustomed to in Cookham Chapel, nor indeed as in the case of our brother Sydney's conversion after hearing an actor (Mr. Quentin Ashley), testify at Maidenhead. The Bible habit in our family was now compellingly re-inforced for Stan by the example of the Old Masters, and by Sydney himself.

Sydney was the brother immediately older than Stan in the family. He was destined for the Church, but instead was killed on the Western Front, before he could be decorated with the M.C. All the time Stan was at the Slade, Sydney was either working to get into Oxford, or up at Oxford, and his concentrated reading had a most stimulating influence on Stan's mind and feelings. Not only the Bible, but Shakespeare, John Donne and 'Urn Burial' buzzed about my ears at bedtime. I remember Stan telling me that he had buried a little tin with a drawing in it down Mill Lane, and 'John Donne arriving in Heaven' was another result of these nightly discussions. The influence of a younger brother was more in the direction of football on the moor, but I also contributed to one of his early pictures. I saw Teddy Wakeling mending cowls on the Maltings, and modelled one myself. It was beautifully made, clinker built, and I erected it on the wall so that I could see it working, until one of our special sou'westers blew it away. Stan's reaction was his famous painting 'Mending Cowls'.

My memory of this time is borne out by Sydney himself in the diary he kept from 1911–1915. He describes sitting for Stan while reading from Job or Milton and beginning *Keats' Letters*, together on Easter Day 1911, and continuing to read them in the train on their way up to Paddington next day. 'Stan and I talked late in bed', is a constant entry—about Bach, Michelangelo, the character of Christ, John Inglesant and so on—and it is nothing extraordinary to read 'To bed with Stan at 10.15. He read *The Tempest*, and I read *Othello*'. But such high-powered concentration is tempered by cheerful accounts of family life when 'Stan solemnly filled coal scuttles, and water-jugs, and made beds with my help', or went walnut bashing from the top of Mr. Parson's shed, 'getting caught by him, and sworn at'.

Light-hearted incidents such as this closely precedes the serious business of the 'Apple Gatherers'. On January 4th 1912, Sydney wrote, 'Stan got on very well with his painting. The group seems to be more substantial. He has covered the neck of the lowest figure with a long curl which has redeemed that head to my fancy'. And on the next day, 'Stan got on with his picture during the whole morning while I read out *Richard Feverel* to him. He is now engaged upon the head of the chief woman figure'. He used his own arm in the glass as a model for hers, and on January 6th, 'he is now on the heads of the four men taking his own mouth in the glass as a copy. He went on with his work till just after 3, when a pupil came'. The arrival of a pupil would, of course, mean that Stan, who was painting in the corner of our dining-room where the piano lived, would quietly lay down his brushes to suit Will's or Father's convenience. Perhaps it was no bad thing, for consequently, 'Stan, Percy and I went down Odney and nearly ran our legs off'.

There was never a day's let up between finishing one picture and starting another. Perhaps it was because of the interruptions downstairs, as well as on account of the better light, that he lashed his 'Self Portrait' on a rickety old easel at the bottom of our bed. In matters of art Sydney did not regard himself as an authority, so it is amusing that he wrote 'In the privacy of one's diary it is surely legitimate to say how much I admire Stan's "Self Portrait", now finished. It is to me nothing short of a masterpiece. And he has done the whole of it with penny hairbrushes.'

Yet with these pictures, now openly acclaimed as masterpieces, leaning against our bedroom wall, Stan's individuality did not make his life at the Slade altogether easy. Sydney's diary for January 18th 1912 reports, 'To bed at 11, and Stan and I had a good hard romp, and then talked about his work at the Slade. Poor chap—he has a bad time of it sometimes'. There is the story of his being put in a sack upside down, and coming back to Cookham with a nose-bleed. But he did not always get the worst of it, although his small stature allied to his quick tongue must have often invited attack. Nevinson was unwise enough to fall out with him when he had on a new suit and Stan squeezed white paint down his back. Before Nevinson could round on him, Stan dropped like a stone to the floor, grabbed Nevinson round the ankles and shackled him. At home he had his own subtle methods of needling his brothers. He pasted a pig's head out of an agricultural magazine over Percy's face in the family group which hung in the dining-room, and waited to see how long it would take for anyone to notice it. Muirhead Bone, who bought Stanley's early picture 'Elizabeth and Zacharias', told me, 'Art is a very indiscreet profession', and I agree with him that there is a certain venom in the expression of the angel striking Zacharias dumb, but I remember Stan had great difficulty with it. Zacharias is burning incense by the Monkey Puzzle tree in the garden of St. George's Lodge. Stan showed me this particular tree later over the wall of 'Wisteria' next door. The concrete wall was a suntrap, and being a little arched at the top, did service for a kind of temple. The man with the branch is wearing a cape of my mother's which was fashionable then.

Almost invariably the key to his paintings are our experiences at home. My interpretation of 'Husband and Wife' (in the possession of Roger Mynors), which some see as cruelly misshapen, is that it represents the triumph of love over every physical disadvantage. We had a cousin so dwarfed that her head scarcely reached above our table. She was the victim of the tragedy of the 'dear Aunt Emma' of our prayers, who returning one Sunday from church, pregnant at the time, found her home burnt down and her husband vanished. Amy, always dressed in black, used to come to Sunday tea with us at intervals, and the tea party usually ended with my father going to the piano and playing 'The King of Love my Shepherd is', while Amy stood at his elbow and sang. If he did not shed a tear, we knew he was much moved. Children are swift to catch the mood, and sympathy and understanding of Amy's feelings flowed from us naturally.

It is this same sympathy and feeling that is expressed in an extraordinary degree in 'Husband and Wife'. They are out for their Sunday evening walk the same as anyone else. They are in their best clothes. She has dolled herself up, her hair is frizzed, her shoes and stockings are touchingly smart. Her arm, sensitively elongated, stretches right across to his heart—the heart of her husband. The picture shocked, as though expositions of this kind are better left to the written word, but to my mind Stan converted the deeper feelings of handicapped people into a physical reality with complete success.

There were a number of strange characters in Cookham in our young days, as there was no question then of placing them in institutions. They were as much benefactors as beneficiaries to the village, teaching us intuitively to be tolerant, and not to tease, which could cause them real anguish of mind. In addition, in time to come Stan almost unconsciously used them as figures in his pictures, particularly the later ones. On our walks with Annie it was nothing unusual to come on Fred Ducket being led by, rather than leading, a horse back to its stable, or Sidney Plum, whose life revolved round the barrel organ, and most exciting of all were the explosive contortions of Miss Mignon Jay, a victim of acute St. Vitus's Dance, but Annie, turning round and catching us staring, would call us off. If, as Mr. Eric Newton wrote, 'Stan never surprised Gil', it is perhaps because I recognize so many of the figures in his pictures. St. Francis always reminds me of Miss Mignon Jay having one of her attacks, her arms thrashing, and her head twisting at right angles. After all St. Francis is said to have been a little 'strange'.

This is the picture that marks a falling off in my brother's judgment, not merely because I have come to think its success as a painting is questionable, but because it exposed a weakness for publicity which, from then on, he unhappily never lost. Initially the design had been for a Chatto & Windus *Almanac*, of Hilda sitting on a haycock reading in a farmyard with a set of rather absurd toy birds in the foreground. Now the fatal figure of Patricia Preece squatting on the right has edged her way in and when Stan removed Hilda on her haycock to introduce St. Francis, he wanted the same weight and shape as he had before, hence the bulky figure of the saint, wrapped in a dressing gown which Ursula and I had taken to Stan in hospital. Recently the Deputy Director of the Tate Gallery and I traced the outline of the original haycock, and there was no doubt about it.

Sir William Llewellyn, the then President of the R.A., was perfectly in his rights to refuse the picture, but Stan's reaction, to resign from the Academy, brought the gossip columnists to his door with pencils sharpened and notebooks out when they found themselves on to a gold mine. Stan not only put it all down, he poured it all out. Noel Carrington meeting me asked, 'Is Stan still spilling the beans?' I said, 'My God he is'.

This was the time in my brother's life when he made his greatest mistake. I believe it would never have happened had Hilda's health held. She was with him throughout his great period of painting before and after Burghclere, bore him two daughters, and though never really able to take responsibility for their household, Stan was prosperous enough to afford the faithful Elsie who was one in a million, and also a rather large Swiss lady, whom he referred to as 'Miss Swiss Alps', who drove the car. No one at that time came between Stan and Hilda, nor in the long run did anyone succeed in doing so. Years later coming away from Hilda's graveside Stan said to me, 'I shall miss her comments'. She was and remained the most powerful force in his life.

In 1932 after completing the murals for the chapel, about which I wrote fully in my first book, the family returned to Cookham to a house called 'Lindworth' which Stan had triumphantly bought, and from which he wrote to me, 'You must just pop down and see this place the first chance you get. It's all too marvellous, and art only can express it', and in the postscript he added, 'It's coming home after a walk that is marvellous in Cookham. Can't you just imagine it, my God! In the kitchen there is a sort of switch indicator, and under in gold letters, W. Bailey, fitter, Cookham'.

But it was not to stay 'too marvellous' for long. Patricia Preece was also at Cookham waiting in the wings. Dick Carline has described her as a person who knew how to flatter. She also had a certain social standing. Years later Stan said if men could strut about like peacocks, they would rid themselves innocuously of their innate vanity. Patricia appealed to his vanity. Since she was already living with her life's companion, Dorothy Hepworth, and wrote disparaging letters about Stan to Roger Fry long before marrying him, he can only have appealed to her as a source of income. From the day of the marriage 'the chain was on the door', as Stan said to me, nor I believe had she ever had any intention to take it off. None the less she kept a tight hold on his purse and property, did up Lindworth extravagantly at his expense, sold it over his head, helped herself to his drawings and exploited the sorry pass to which she had brought him. Creative genius when it breaks down after great strain can turn rancid. The birth of God's greatest creation is chucked in a bucket. In the case of my brother the aftermath has been preserved as the main interest of certain types of minds.

Driving through a village near Bury St. Edmunds lately I saw a poster advertising a popular Sunday paper, with a greatly enlarged excellent photograph of my brother taken by *Picture Post* when he was making his marvellous drawings up at Glasgow for his ship-building 'War' pictures. On this occasion it was simply labelled in huge letters 'Stanley Spencer' on the top, and underneath 'The Evil Genius'. The Sunday paper in question was serializing excerpts from Miss Collis' recent book which records Patricia's view of Stanley, not to be published, of course, till after her death. After reading it, Mary Behrend wrote to me in no uncertain terms as to where the evil lay. Had Miss Collis, or her father before her, cared to consult old friends like the Behrends, or members of Stan's immediate family, their books might have given a more balanced account of Stanley's domestic tragedy.

Its immediate affect was to leave him not only comfortless, but reduced to extreme poverty, compared to his prosperity when with Hilda. Dudley Tooth took over complete control of Stan's affairs for the rest of his life, but could only allow him £2 pocket money a week at first, which slowly rose to £4, and only grew to £10 a week, in the fifties. Always the pressure was on him to produce pictures of a quick saleable kind, and I remember seeing him on Paddington Station when he was at the height of his fame holding out one of his 'pot boilers' at arms' length because it was still wet saying, 'Dudley wants it in a hurry'. At the same time Mr. Wilfred Evill, Stan's solicitor, was able to acquire the largest collection of Stan's figure paintings in private hands.

Happily Stan retained an utter indifference to his affairs and though his personal problems remained insoluble, he was able to escape from his pre-occupation with them by being commissioned by the Ministry of Information as a War Artist. In the summer of 1940 he first went to Glasgow to make drawings for his famous shipyard paintings. When Percy saw him off at Euston and asked him had he any money, he had only the change from his ticket in his pocket. None the less it suited him to live in simple lodgings with a footballer-blacksmith and his wife, and he wrote he was having 'a grand time at the Port'. He was mixing with people who best understood him and took his talk with a grain of salt, which was so often an enigma to intellectuals, misjudged by gossips, and feared by the respectable. In a letter he wrote to me in 1942 he complained that, 'anything I say nowadays—doesn't matter what it is, "Nice day", anything, a look of apprehension comes into the face of the listener. They seize the back of a chair for support. I have to calm them down first, and say, "Now, it's all right, I am only going to say it's a nice day!" Perhaps in view of my more pithy statements that would be a bit of a shock. Up at the Port sometimes when I had let fly to a considerable extent on my more peculiar views—you know the sort of thing "I'm married to everybody really in varying degrees" etc. etc. Joe, the boxing champion looks up from poking the fire, and, in a quiet voice says, "Yee'l go oot on your nut".'

Describing his drawings for the 'Glasgow Resurrection' in 1944 he explained that the group of mourners filling the top left corner of his picture and looking at the contents of a tomb in the shape of an open book was taken originally from 'a drawing I did of myself showing one of my big books of sketches to the chaps in the shipyards. I and others held it, and let the pages flop down before the admiring hundreds of shipyard chaps and girls'. In the same letter he described his drawing for the old man who 'crawls from an open square tomb from the right hand into the centre part of the picture where he meets his old wife, she crawling from her right hand half of the picture to do so. They both face each other in a state of wonder and delight. "Wherever have you been all this long come short?" I like the feeling that this left side of the picture is the male wing, and on the right of centre is the female wing, like Bristol Asylum. The girl striding out from the same tomb to the left centre is meeting her sailor husband on whose grave she had placed large sea shells as they do, you remember.'

I notice that in the margin of this letter about his 'Glasgow Resurrection' I have written in block capitals, 'No Sign of Lack of Vision Here'. In his introduction to the catalogue of his retrospective exhibition at the Tate in 1955 he wrote of his fear that he was losing his vision. My feeling is that he no doubt lost the first rapture that came to him in early days, but his vision was still there. It seems to me his failure was in the colour, and that he buried the beauty of his line and of the first tonal washes by covering his figures with checks and patterns to counteract what had become his inability to deal with form. But if anything there was still an overcrowding of ideas, as Tonks had predicted long ago, rather than a loss of imagination.

Stan himself has written about that wonderful series of 'Resurrection' pictures which, could they have been collected together, would have filled a building as large as Burghclere Chapel. Louis Behrend, that 'peach of patrons' as Henry Lamb described him, was the only man to give Stan the chance to complete and unify his ideas. Shame that in spite of that extraordinary achievement, no trust or public body, let alone private person, ever again gave him a similar opportunity. True that in some cases it was his own fault. He was the worst person in the world to handle managements or committees. Louis Behrend, with Henry Lamb to hand, came straight on to Stan's marvellous and clear-sighted designs in single tone wash, and knew exactly what he was commissioning. The architect too could plan the building to the scale required by the drawings. But in the case of Llandaff Cathedral where Stan hoped to paint a 'Last Judgment', and was acutely disappointed when nothing came of it, he travelled up to Llandaff to lunch with the Canons without plans or drawings to show them, whereas Epstein who was well-versed in procuring commissions, had 'Christ in Glory' in the guard's van. Stan might have hoped for better luck at Coventry where an £80,000 trust fund, held by the Academy, was on the doorstep, but those in a position to commission him did not do so.

Meanwhile his head was full of another vast undertaking, his 'Christ at Cookham Regatta', and again he was to be faced with the same frustrations; no patron, no building, and the perennial demand from Messrs. Tooth for flower pictures and landscapes. Poor little beggar! his head teeming with ideas, having to carry them all around with him. I regard his 'Chapel to Women', with which he occupied himself in his loneliness, as an off-shoot of the suppression he suffered from not being able to paint what he longed to paint. 'I never get anything done nowadays', he wrote in 1957. 'Being called away to do some landscape (and I have to think I am lucky to have such work offered me), is so *not* what I intend, that it disturbs me in doing the work I *do* want and love to do.' Had he only been given a chapel as at Burghclere in which to concentrate upon his heaven on earth (where else would Christ come if not to Cookham?), his mind would have been settled and his imagination fully extended.

My first sight of 'Christ preaching at Cookham Regatta' was in that most unlikely of studios, his bedroom at Cliveden View. Ursula and I were on one of our routine visits which were always carefully planned, and confirmed by him by postcard, or from the telephone kiosk nearby. Stan holding his palette in one hand greeted us at the door, and we entered against an array of boxes and other minor obstacles which he kicked out of our way as we followed him upstairs. There we saw a large canvas rolled up and nailed on to his bedroom wall, leaving some of it exposed down the centre on which he was working, gradually unfurling it as he progressed.

At first we stood or sat about talking of 'Christ

preaching at Cookham' quite naturally as though it was a most usual event. With so little of the picture to go on I was puzzled at first, but having returned from lunch at the 'Copper Kettle' things began to move and I could understand his excitement. Adopting his usual position, something between squatting and kneeling, he dealt out on to the floor sheaves of drawings which he proceeded to fit together so that we could see what the picture was going to be like on completion. The drawings were beautiful, and of course without colour. I say thank God he never completed the painting, for we are left with something of the beauty of the original line still showing in the unfinished parts.

Just as at Burghclere the side walls of the chapel are occupied by ordinary happenings at the hospital or in camp, so now he had planned happenings at Cookham regatta for the side walls of the chapel, a number of which he succeeded in painting like 'Punts Meeting' or 'Dinner on Ferry Hotel Lawn' even 'Sarah Tubb and the Heavenly Visitors', but these had to be sold separately. 'Christ preaching' on which he was now working, was for the altar piece of course. Instead of his favourite pitched up aspects as at Burghclere, when by climbing an imaginary ladder he could change his own elevation, thereby indulging effectively the eye of his imagination to the full, I could see that this time his view of Christ was from the flat of Bell Rope Meadow, not much above the water table. He told me he was having trouble with the perspective of the pleasure steamer *May Queen* which had tied up alongside and was in the way of the figure of Christ. By scraping out most of the hull he lowered it behind the bank out of the way. I saw what he had done when I noticed the dust on the floor below it and though I did not jump to it at the time, it was the writing on the wall. Always he had been almost maddeningly strict about sticking to the original drawings. That something should go wrong after he had started to paint would have been to him akin to horror. He would lower his voice referring to such a happening, and from the time he started to draw his ideas 'all out of m' own head' on to the paper, I rarely remember his rubbing out or altering.

The writing was on the wall too in the strange insistence of inaccurate details such as the graining on the side of the punts and he substituted the beautiful bowsprit of the *Queen*, which had been in the way, by an absurd attempt to invent one with no practical meaning. He seemed obsessed and caught up in complications of the sort even though passionately anxious to finish the painting, hopping in and out of his camp bed at any time of day or night to paint a little more, and neglectful of the pain that increasingly attacked him. As animals return to their grazing the minute the pain has gone, so did my brother to his 'Christ preaching'. But the time came when in the early hours of one morning the pain finally took over. He described, having failed to rouse his sleeping neighbours by shouting for help, he thought how the sound of his name might come to them and shouted 'Stanley Spencer is ill', adding dramatically how he heard their footsteps as they ran from their cottages across the road, and round the corner.

From then on, in between hospital treatment, he would carry the huge canvas of 'Christ preaching at Cookham', rolled up about with him wherever he was convalescing. The last time I saw Stan working on it he climbed up on to a chair on top of a table calling down, 'If you want to see what I am doing you will have to come up here'. He pointed out his appallingly vulgar landlord on the lawn of the Ferry Hotel and said that he had 'pinched' him from my 'Miller' whom I had painted at Lemsford leaning on a post gazing across the stream, a lonely and brightly romantic figure. Stan's landlord was a complete negation of my approach. On the other hand I was intrigued to notice that the ladies in the punt wore dresses astonishingly accurate to the period, and it came to my mind that we used to see Dorothy Bailey's designs for a fashion house in London, mixed in with Mr. Bailey's wallpaper books, and undoubtedly Stan had made use of these.

He was a dying man when he was summoned to the Palace to be knighted. The Queen Mother, speaking slowly, said, as she dubbed him, 'I have been waiting to do this for a long time'.

20

Walsham-le-Willows

BEFORE I left Upper Basildon, Lord Alastair Gordon introduced me to a director of Massey Ferguson with the idea that I should paint a picture to advertise their machines. I did a series of cameos illustrating the progress of husbandry spreading them across a landscape which I had already in mind, and placing them where I felt I wanted them. On the left I painted an ancient Briton scratching the earth with seagulls settling round him, and below my idea of the Tolpuddle Martyrs remonstrating with their master. In the centre of the picture was a horse-drill being covered up for the last time, and the horses, unharnessed, being led away. As I moved to the right the inevitable Massey Ferguson appeared ploughing into the jungle, driving the wild animals before it.

I was so happy painting this picture (later bought by the Chantry Bequest) that I almost ran down the path each morning to get on with it, and it would have been unthinkable to me at the time that I should ever decide to leave Tree Cottage. Only a year before, in 1969, I had persuaded my kind neighbour to build a lovely wooden fence for me, along the entire frontage, based on a photograph of what had been there originally. My friends stopped to admire it and were reassured when I said I was certainly not 'tarting up' Tree Cottage to sell it. Nothing was further from my thoughts then. True, on a visit to my friends in Suffolk in the spring of 1970 I was offered the refusal of a cottage which was being modernized but I did not take the suggestion seriously. A week later on my return to Basildon, my brother Percy died, and with him the last link with my family, and the whole of my past life.

It was Percy, with my sister Florence, who made a reality of Fernley for us when the crash came. She went away as a governess; he was taken away from school and put to work in Bourne End giving half his earnings to Father. I was reminded how careful he was on our behalf when Stan wrote to me in August '57 saying, 'I went and saw Perce yesterday. He was delighted to have his memory refreshed in respect of a Funeral Policy (twopence a week) which he took out for you and me when we were about ten and eleven years of age. It was against our burial he said.' I remember the awful feeling we both had, that for some reason we were different from normal people, and must be provided against some horrible 'hitch'. Certainly Percy was another of those 'pebbles to be found on the shingly stream down Odney', another essential if sleeping partner in the emergence of Stan's genius. At Percy's funeral which few attended I whispered to Gillian that there might well have been no laurel wreaths, no muffled bells for Stanley, but for the part Percy played both in Stan's early life, and in the dark period after Hilda's breakdown and Patricia's treachery, when he was living alone in a desolate room in Adelaide Road, going out for his food, and bringing in coal in small bags for heating. Percy, who found him painting some paper flowers for Tooth's, took him out and bought him a great-coat of which Stan was very proud, and afterwards fixed him up in Cliveden View up Cookham Rise, never for a moment thinking he would stay there. But it suited Stan, he said there were 'too many rooms in Fernley', Cliveden View was only just big enough for himself.

Now with Percy's death Tree Cottage suddenly seemed too big and lonely for me. I rang up the Martineaus at Walsham-le-Willows and said I would take their cottage. Soon after, towards midnight while writing at my table in the normal way, I was seized with some kind of frenzy that if I did not begin to move then and there I might change my mind and not go at all. I kept eyeing the sofa which I knew would be too large to move, but I did not know what it would be like smashing up a sofa in an otherwise orderly sitting-room. Had anyone looked through the window they might have feared I had gone raving mad as I swung the axe at the sofa's prostrate form lying like some beast of the jungle at my feet. Terrifying! Every time I tried to pull out its ribs they did some kind of double twist back into a belly full of tightly packed horsehair. I only recovered some sort of sanity about 3 a.m. when I looked at the wall just above where the sofa had been to see my John Nash, Rodney Burn, and Percy Horton looking as serene and peaceful as ever, to re-assure me.

Soon the village could have had no doubt of my intention to leave as the most almighty bonfires began to blaze away behind Tree Cottage, on which I flung some of the past, but none of the future. Ursula and I had spent nearly the whole of our married life in Upper Basildon, and over the years had gained and thoroughly reciprocated the affection of the village. We felt ourselves personalities among personalities, and I became much exercised in my mind as to how I should take my leave.

With a characteristic sense of occasion I saw myself as a guest at a farewell party in the Village Hall, which as is usual in village life, was the centre of social occasions of every kind. Gillian and Shirin, my niece, with Margaret Miles took part in a concert for the Artists' General Benevolent Institution there, and there were the usual bazaars and raffles for enlarging the hall, or building a new church, which attracted pictures from me. I remember Mrs. Messenger's expression as she was coming away with an appalling clock saying, 'Where on earth am I going to hang this?' I knew what I would have liked her to have to hang, but it was won by one of the richest men in the village for half a crown.

Now, in anticipation of my 'farewell party' I planned how I would slip down to the hall in the morning and hide a 40 inches by 30 inches canvas 'Upper Basildon from the Old Pump House' behind the curtain on the stage, and thought of what I would say in my speech. It would be brief, and sincere, without notes, and as I spoke I would edge towards the curtain, and drawing it back would ask the Chairman of the Parish Council, with whom I had, as a member, not always agreed (laughter) to accept it on behalf of the village as a reminder of the many years and happy times we had spent there.

But there was no party! When Land's furniture van backed into the gate Joyce and I had made such a splendid job of packing up, that all my worldly goods were carted in and away in a couple of hours including my 'rejected address'—the picture I never had the opportunity to present. Of far greater importance, also in the van, was a precious canvas 'The Rick Party, Commem Week' which I had struggled with for a long time, and which was I believed at last 'pinned down'. It was with relief that I unpacked it again, unharmed, in the old nursery at Brook Farm, Walsham-le-Willows, which until my cottage was ready for me became my studio. Ursula and I had spent our last holiday together there, so that I felt very much at home and found myself as naturally running across the road to Brook Farm as I used to run down the path to my studio at Basildon.

'The Rick Party' was one of those ideas that had come back at me for forty years, but in spite of variations I had never satisfied myself. The occasion was one of the many parties I enjoyed with the Drysdales in the '20s, when they lived in a mysterious house just outside Abingdon called Wick Hall. I had taught Enid Drysdale at the Ruskin School of Drawing. She used to wait for me at the Lodge gates, and we bicycled together to Oxford, and on Sunday nights I would bicycle over from Spring Road to join the family party. On the evening of the picnic, we drove in a car, which like most cars in those days was the worse for wear, till we found ourselves in a rick yard. I liked the feeling of it, but was not thinking of a picture then. We perched ourselves around old bales of hay and loose straw, and spread our picnic on top, and a young man, a toff, in a white tie on his way to a commem ball made an effective impression on top of the rick against the approaching sunset, and an impression of another kind on me because he was making himself agreeable to a girl in the party, whom I knew and liked very much. For a long time after that evening the feeling of that picnic 'visited' me, and I kept on seeing in my mind's eye the group of girls, one plunging her arms into a basket, another flinging the cloth across, and a third, reaching out, but not quite reaching, the plate that was being passed to her. Had she been able to reach it it would have put a brake on the movement which was the last thing I wanted. But I had had great trouble with myself stretched across the foreground, and I funked it until after many visits to the National Gallery I determined that if Seurat could do it in his 'Bathers' why couldn't

I? In the happy and homely atmosphere of the children's nursery at Brook Farm, visited and encouraged by the family who had grown up there, at last I brought it off.

I had been at Walsham just eight months when I put the finishing touch to the 'Rick Party' and packed it off to the Academy. In celebration I shared a wonderful invitation from the vicar and his sister, John and Rosemary Rutherford, to visit Chartres from door to door. We left Walsham at 5.30 a.m. on Easter Monday morning (1971) in their remarkable old Bentley, and were supping at the Boeuf Couronné in the Square at Chartres punctually at 8 p.m. that evening. Next morning when I woke and gazed across in the early light at those grey towers I thought had I died in my sleep a more heavenly shroud could not have been prepared for me.

I had been to Chartres once before with Ursula returning from a visit to Brother Will at Thün. We had broken our journey in Paris and made a typically 'Perfidious Albion' day trip to Chartres, when instead of making a bee line for the cathedral we thought it could wait till we had had lunch. Looking up from our cutlets we saw a colossal black queue of people slowly processing across the square summoned to the cathedral by a single tolling bell, and were told by our Mademoiselle that it was the funeral of a Noterie Publique. I could see at a glance that if we did not join the queue at once we would never get into the cathedral at all. Actually when we reached the gaping doors we stepped to one side, and praying for a short service, spent the time looking at the cathedral from outside. When at last we were able to enter, I was not equipped to appreciate the beauty of the glass, but the impact to one's feelings remained. Now with Rosemary, an eminent stained glass artist, ready to share her expert knowledge and enthusiasm, the windows were lit up for me even more clearly. Her description of the subtleties and vital importance of the leading was an added joy to me, and to some extent explained her skill in following the map on our journey through France. Her brother drove faultlessly and without question. He knew she would never miss a turning.

On our last evening in Chartres we went to a little restaurant where I lowered the standards of the party by saying too loudly 'Vive la France', in a Churchillian accent, but it was surely better than referring to them as those b— frogs as we used to call them in Salonika. On our way back to our hotel we wandered into the cathedral just to have a last look, and stood transfixed in the dim light of the nave by the singing of a choir from Aix-la-Chapelle. It was a moving farewell.

For the rest of the trip I chiefly remember being asphyxiated at Blois and drinking tap water at Alençon which nearly killed me, so that our visit to the Bayeux Tapestry was a very mixed occasion for me. But I recovered in time for one of the most profound ex-experiences of the holiday, the sight of the ruins of the abbey at Joumièges.

Church Rise Cottage was ready for me at last in July 1971 including a little studio tucked to one side just large enough to hold my ancient tallboys, every cranny of which is stuffed with bits and pieces of drawings carelessly pushed into it over the years. But painting since I came here has had to give way to writing, aware though I am that my father would turn a complete sommersault in his grave at the thought of my daring to write, not one, but two books. Will's tone of voice and gesture, as he said, 'Good Gracious, Gilbert, don't *you* start being serious', comes to me across the years. They didn't take into account that the last shall be last.

Meanwhile my studio does not go unvisited. People come and go, turning over crumpled drawings and fragments of ideas, smoothing them out, and often carrying them off to frame as if they had suddenly become important. Not that I would ever deny that I am not a draughtsman of a generation that held drawing to be a major joy of the Fine Art. Some of my drawings are comic, partly because as Will knew, I have always found the comic irresistible, but also because in comic drawings one gains a freedom of style which is a good exercise for more serious drawing. Stan in fact never made a comic drawing, but that is not to say he did not enjoy mine. Somewhere there is the drawing I did for him when he had been asked to open an exhibition in Birmingham in January 1956, and because he had a bad throat he had told them 'Get Gil'. I wrote to describe the occasion, and added a drawing in which I imagined Stan in the audience with a gag over his mouth, such as, as children, we had thought people wore, not for hygienic reasons, but because they were dumb.

Stan answered, 'I love the drawing of me with the gag on my mouth, and the mayor is grand, typical *Lord* Mayor, not just mayor . . . You get very good stuff out of these sorts of visits. It seems a funny thing to me that while neither of us paint to compensate ourselves for being dumb, and we both have the gift of speech (at least I had until I recently took the gag) yet in all these talks I never remember seeing anyone taking the talk down verbatim. The drawing of me in the stalls among the gentry, and you with arm easily flung out, sort of à la "St. Francis appears at Arles" is so true. I notice the way my head turns *full* sideways: I am a bit afraid of people especially the type of man sitting next to me in your drawing, and my fear makes me give him all the attention I feel he will expect, and more in case he needs it. This results in a false attentiveness, and the stupid turn of the head. But our friend sitting next to me! *Where* do these sort of men, worthies of the City of Birmingham, and everywhere else, get their colossal *assurance* from? You notice in the drawing that he does *not* turn his head, or hardly, but just eases round a bit to see if he can tolerate a glimpse of this monstrosity sitting next to him. There is no getting upsides with it. I give myself pep talks, "You've done very well, Stanley, and you are just as good as that chap next to you, possibly better . . . but it makes no difference."'

I quote this letter because it describes our sense of inferiority of never having got 'upsides with' what I call 'Eton, Harrow, Winchester'—effortless superiority, and at the same time our resentment of it. We were all 'different' but Stanley was the most different of us all, so perhaps he felt it most keenly. In one of his last letters to me, written on May 19th 1959, when he had become a prophet in his own country, he wrote, 'While people are ready to accord me praise for the reputation I have achieved they are determined not to seek any such thing themselves. There is a chap at Cookham Rise who catches the 7.35 every morning. He is nonchalant but determinedly so, no hat, balding, rolled umbrella swung in don't-care way: he is resolved and determined he's *not* going to set the Thames on fire, let the silly so and so's try it who wish. With every extra wave of news about me you can see him dig his heels in, and give an extra tightening twist to the umbrella. One feels they have all had such a hell of a scramble to get from life anything approaching the common decencies, that having secured that damn roof over their heads they are going to lay low. These wealthy people have found refuge in the houses in the village. They are right on the street, but not in it. I shall have to start the basket-arm-chair-sit-in-front-garden-summer-evening-style.'

Walsham like Cookham has changed since I first knew it but is still full of character. Even so, as a painter I do not care for Suffolk—it is too flat, and the farms of today with their cold steel sheds and cows, all of the same colour, each with a bedside light at night, and *The Times* provided with their breakfast, would have killed my farm pictures stone dead. Yet, thanks to the Martineau family who have massed to help me, I feel at home. Just a few steps 'up the rise' is not only the church, but the 'Six Bells', and from my kitchen window looking across Gallant's Meadow I can see the roof of my Right Hand—a second Joyce, who to my rescue came. She has polished me up so much that I am in danger of becoming the sort of toff Stan so much disliked. Moreover since the birth of my grandson Glyn Spencer Hopkins in November 1972, there can be no man alive, be he Eton, Harrow or Winchester, with a greater feeling of 'effortless superiority'. I hope to go walking and talking, Spencer fashion, hand-in-hand with him before completing 'Lord now lettest'.

For some long while now I have accepted cheerfully a seven day week. The bells of St. James' from high pitched Shaftesbury were not answered by my laying down of brushes. Yet how I loved those bells, and want the churches. For me their doors are not closed. I am still at home at Evensong with a friend when I am not ruffled by dogma and creeds. One miserable afternoon in the rain I came on a little church hidden away near Oxford Station, and went in. It was very dark. Looking towards the sharp light outside through the half open door I saw a number of tombs tottering with age into their graves. I was happy and settled. Not knowing does not mean not feeling.

APPENDIX

Brother Stan

by Eric Newton

GILBERT and Stanley Spencer were more than brothers. They were affinities. Their means of communication with each other was by a kind of shorthand in which signs, inflexions of the voice hardly detectable to outsiders, fleeting facial expressions, the almost monosyllabic interchanges that crystallize into a secret family language took the place of the normally elaborate verbal conversation between normally intelligent human beings.

In *Stanley Spencer* (Victor Gollancz), written and illustrated by Gilbert Spencer, this closeness is never stated or described. It is implicit. And the result is a book of such disarming simplicity that one begins to absorb, as one reads, the grammar of this secret language. It has the essence, especially in boyhood, of the relationship between two brothers who were also two artists, and who instinctively, as well as affectionately, understood each other. Gilbert has written, probably unconsciously, a book permeated by this kind of family shorthand.

In writing this chatty, discursive, brief yet leisurely chronicle, full of little chuckles and jokes and anecdotes, Gilbert Spencer has found it necessary to describe not only his brother's progress from childhood to adolescence and then onwards to success and fame, and an incidental knighthood, but also the whole closely knit texture of life within the framework of a large family. Equally inevitably, there had to be a frame outside the frame describing life in Cookham-on-Thames. For the Spencers belonged, quite alarmingly, to Cookham. To a little Stanley the village was the whole world in miniature. And, in the end, Cookham belonged to Stanley. He turned it into a legend by assuming that everything in Cookham was of the utmost importance, from a conversation in the grocer's shop to the idea that Christ could carry his cross through the streets of Cookham, that he should preach to the villagers from a punt in Cookham Regatta and that the Resurrection should take place in Cookham churchyard. For what made Stanley Spencer a great painter was partly his conviction that painting was synonymous with autobiography; and partly an innocent mysticism. Autobiography was as much concerned with the unseen as with the seen.

All this his brother doubtless realized when he wrote this book; yet it is quite deliberately a book not about an artist but a brother whose name throughout is 'Stan', just as his own is 'Gil'. There were other brothers—William, George, Harold, Percy Julius, and Sydney: there were sisters—Annie and Florence: and there was father—an intelligent eccentric—and mother—a wise and sensible angel. And although Stan, from first to last, is always in focus and always somewhere near the book's centre, the family's comings and goings never cease to be of the restless and lively composition that revolves round him. It must have been the oddest family, unworldly, innocent, quite unaware of fashionable ways of thinking and talking, but gifted with a brilliance that, in Stanley's case, amounted to genius.

* * *

Later, as Stan grows up, outsiders edge their way in—

Henry Lamb, Lady Ottoline Morrell, Hilda Carline who became Stan's wife, Louis and Mary Behrend who made one of the most enlightened gestures in the history of recent patronage when they built the memorial chapel at Burghclere, and commissioned Stan to fill it with the murals that are the most important that twentieth-century England has produced.

What Gilbert Spencer has to say about Stan's way of painting (usually in the corner of a crowded room or squatting on the floor) is fascinating: and when he describes the workings of Stan's creative mind, he is brilliantly illuminating. Yet the illumination always seems to occur in a casual parenthesis. It is not the book's purpose to explain Stanley but to describe him. Other authors will doubtless produce detailed critical biographies. They will be needed, for the roots of Spencer's genius were buried in the soil of his lovable personality. A special key and a rather rare kind of vision are needed for an acceptance of the deeper levels of his art. That vision and that key Gilbert Spencer possesses almost unconsciously. But in this book he has hardly bothered to use them. He could write another book—an interpretation rather than a biography—but it would not be as gay or as intimate or as affectionate or as unassuming as this.

One almost dreads the laboriously penetrating analyses of the art of Sir Stanley Spencer that will one day be published. And one knows that compared with this careless overflow of reminiscence, they will be incomplete. Only a Spencer could know what another Spencer is made of. I think I knew Stanley fairly well, but he never failed to surprise me. Stan never surprised Gil, and that is why Gil's book about Stan is a delight.

Index

INDEX